L.T. Frog

L.T. Frog

Learning to FULLY RELY ON GOD

REBECCA K. BROWN

Outskirts Press, Inc.
Denver, Colorado

The opinions expressed in this manuscript are solely the opinions of the author and do not represent the opinions or thoughts of the publisher. The author has represented and warranted full ownership and/or legal right to publish all the materials in this book.

L.T. Frog
Learning to Fully Rely on God
All Rights Reserved.
Copyright © 2009 Rebecca K. Brown
v2.0

Cover Photo © 2009 JupiterImages Corporation. All rights reserved - used with permission.

This book may not be reproduced, transmitted, or stored in whole or in part by any means, including graphic, electronic, or mechanical without the express written consent of the publisher except in the case of brief quotations embodied in critical articles and reviews.

Outskirts Press, Inc.
http://www.outskirtspress.com

ISBN: 978-1-4327-3561-6

Outskirts Press and the "OP" logo are trademarks belonging to Outskirts Press, Inc.

PRINTED IN THE UNITED STATES OF AMERICA

Contents

About the Book vii
Acknowledgements ix
Cutting the Clutter 1
Love Is What? 5
Green - A Time to Move Forward 9
Making It Personal! Making It Your Story! 13
How Could God Reject His Only Son? 17
In the Merry Month of May 21
Father Knows Best 25
F.R.O.G. - Fully Rely On God 31
A Summer of Blessings 35
School Days 39
Campfires and Faith 43
A Beautiful Weed 47
What Costume Are You Wearing? 51
November: A Time for Reflection and the Giving of Thanks 55
Christmas of a Different Kind 59
Taking Off the Comfortable and Wearing the Uncomfortable 63
What Is Normal? 67
Me Walk on Water, Are You Kidding? 71
Haiti 75
Sharing Your Faith, What a Breeze 79
What an Awesome God! 83

McVeigh Dies – Judgment Day	87
Finding Calmness in a Hectic World!	91
What Does God Expect From Us?	95
A Personal Relationship—What's Up With That?	99
Are You Prepared for the Celebration?	103
A Deeper Relationship with Christ	107
Dropping Things and Letting Go!	111
Good Stuff or Junk	115
How Do You Communicate?	119
Make Disciples	123
Spiritual Warfare	127
Stages of Life	131
The Cross and the Electric Chair	135
Use All Your Strength – Including Your Father's	139
Peace	143
I Did It Again!	149
Spiritual Therapy: How's Yours?	153
Who Will Be Your "Stitcher" for the Year?	157
God's Blessing	161
Worry? Who Me?	165
Couldn't You Stay Awake?	171
The Passion of the Christ	175
Winter Storm Watch	179
A Frustrating Stain; It Just Won't Go Away	183
Making Disciples	187
Jesus Calms the Storm	193
The Disciples	197
Could You Be a Noah?	201
Dust, Dirt, and Grime	205
God Gave You a Talent: Are You Hiding It?	209
Will and Power	213
More Than a Glass of Water	217
Don't Ask Me to Leave	221
We Don't Always Feel Like Having an Attitude for Gratitude	225
Childhood Games, Not So Fun!	229
Help in Troubled Times	233
Bear One Another's Burdens	237
References	241

About the Book

L. T. Frog, which is the name I chose for this book, stands for *learning to fully rely on God*. That is what this book is all about, a book of devotionals God has inspired me to write. It is for the beginner; it is for those who want to learn to rely on God more fully. These devotionals are not for the Biblical scholar; they are not for the Saints who have led a Godly life. They are for everyday people who live everyday lives. These are for people who struggle with issues on a daily basis.

Some are faith stories and some are learning experiences, but all are inspired by God. Some of these I feel God gave me in the truest sense. I would start an article with a thought or two that He had given me, and He would take it from there. I didn't even know how some of these devotionals would turn out or where He was leading me until the end. I have shared them with many people over the years. I have received many phone calls and notes from friends and family telling me how they have helped them develop a closer, deeper relationship with Christ. I certainly do not take credit. God has so graciously given me this talent, and it is my duty to share it. When people call and thank me because a particular devotion has helped them, I ask them to just thank God that I was willing to be used for *Him* and to thank *Him* for the talent He has given me.

It is my total desire to follow Christ in all ways of my life. It is my total desire to follow Christ every day of my life. I also have a passion to share Christ with others. I do it through my life and my articles. If I can lead people to Christ or help draw them closer to Him, then I praise God that I have done what He has sent me to do. I may only be a seed and someone else may come and water that seed; that is a good thing, too.

My life has been one about struggles, difficult choices, and jumping out of the boat. My prayer is that something I have done, lived through, or struggled with may help each of you live more fully for God.

May God bless each of you as you read these devotionals. I pray they will draw you closer to God and help you *fully rely on God* for all things. I also pray God will put in you the desire to share Christ with others.

In Christian Love,
Becky

Acknowledgements

This book is in memory of my mother. She was my mentor, guide, teacher, and best friend. It is because of her faith I am where I am and doing what I am today. Thanks, Dad, for sticking with Mom through it all. If you two hadn't stuck it out, I wouldn't be here today. We had our ups and downs, but you were always there for Greg and me.

To my loving husband of thirty plus years, Greg, you are the love of my life. Our journey together has been rough, difficult, fun, and exciting. It has taken us places we never even thought about. We have done things we thought were impossible, but with God, all things are possible. Thank you for loving me and always lifting me up, supporting me, and letting me be a little crazy. Thank you for believing in me.

To my three beautiful daughters and their spouses, you are the ones I look to for help, support, and to keep me straight. There are times you keep me up at night wondering what's going on, you keep me laughing, and sometimes you make me cry. I love you all and thank you for encouraging me to do this. To my beautiful son in heaven, I miss you. You are forever in my heart and always on my mind. To my four grandchildren, Memaw loves you very much. You are what keeps me going. I enjoy our times together. Remember to keep the faith and when I can't be with you, God is.

To my brother and sister, thanks for always being there and for your love and friendship. What a great brother and sister to have! To Norm and Lila, thanks for stepping in and being my parents when I lost mine. You have seen me through the difficult times, as well as the fun times. You have helped me in my faith journey. I will always be indebted to you.

To Pastors Scott, Buck, Paul, and Tom, you, too, have all helped me along my faith journey. I have enjoyed working for you and being not only your secretary, but your friend. Thank you for lighting my path along the journey and for being there when I needed you. You were all put in my path for a reason—thanks. Tom, thanks for encouraging me and pushing me to get on the Web.

To Mt. Tabor (Dunkirk, IN) and First United Methodist Church (Burleson, TX) you both are special. Mt. Tabor was there for me as I grew in my faith, and so many of you have blessed my life with your love and friendship. It was an honor to serve as your secretary for twelve years. I became strong in my faith because of you. You wanted to make disciples for Christ and you have succeeded. Thanks! To FUMC, thanks for accepting me and allowing me to become a part of your church family. You have accepted me as I am.

To Nancy, Brenda, Diane and the Seekers Class, I love you! Thanks for being there to listen to me. We are sisters in Christ and I am proud to call you family. To my Emmaus friends, Tana Beth, JoLynn, Vickie, and Selena, you set me straight and hold me accountable for my actions, and I certainly need it. You are a special group of sisters, as well. To my friend, Donna, thanks for pushing me and pushing me. This book has come about because of you. I am not sure I could have done this without you walking alongside me. Thanks, girlfriend!

To Michelle at Outskirts, thanks for your advice and hints along the way; it has been a pleasant experience. To Tiffany at Write Word Edit, we haven't met in person, yet I feel I have found a true friend. It has been a pleasure to get to know you and work with you. Thanks for all your hard work and encouraging words. To Mildred George, thanks for your help as well, you are a dear friend.

I have mentioned a lot of people, but there have been many more who have made a huge impact on my life—you know who you are. I will be forever indebted to those who have walked alongside me, pushed me from the back, and were ahead of me lighting my way. From mission trips to retreats to Bible studies, you have been what I needed when I needed you. Thank you for making this book possible.

To the reader, thank you for purchasing this book. It is for you I write. May God open your heart and mind to the things He wants to share with you. It is all about walking together and helping each other on this journey of life. I hope through something God has shared with me your journey will be made a little easier.

Finally, to God, thank you for believing in me enough to give me a talent where I can share your thoughts and words with others. I have always said you are the author, I am the instrument. May you reap benefits from this book and may you receive all the glory and honor. It's all about you and not me.

Cutting the Clutter

Philippians 1:6, Romans 8:26

Do you know someone who has a really cluttered desk? One of the ministers I worked for had a *really* cluttered desk. What kind of image does that bring to your mind? Disorder, confusion, a real mess is what comes to my mind; how about you? We all made remarks and laughed at his cluttered desk. There were times I would lay things on his desk, and they would be lost. One day I looked at it differently. The question popped into my head, *Am I any different?* Well, today my desk does look messy, but somehow I don't think that was what I was to be thinking about. I don't think God was asking me about my desk. I think He was referring to the clutter in my life. We all have it. We may not admit it, but we all have a certain amount of clutter, and just like those people who have cluttered desks we need to stop and clean the clutter and reorganize our own lives. What better time than today to evaluate and clean the clutter?

    Where do we begin cutting the clutter, you ask? What about all those meetings and social events that keep us away from Wednesday night services or a Bible study? How about those late Saturday night evenings that keep us from getting up and going to church or "sleeping" through church? I am guilty of "sleeping" through church (even though my eyes may be open). Then there is that flimsy excuse, "Well, Sundays are my only days to sleep in." My question to you is what if God decided to sleep in the day you needed Him most? Aren't we so busy cluttering our lives with things to do that we can't seem to find time for God? Are our lives so cluttered we can't find time to be alone with God? Many of us find time to read the paper, but not the Bible. We all find time to talk to friends and family, yet many of us can't find the time to pray. Some of us could even be saying, "You're right, but I work hard in the church. I am so busy at church doing things I don't have much time for anything else. When I do find time I don't want to be busy praying or reading the Bible. I want time for me."

Reality check here: We cannot earn our way to Heaven. Staying busy doing all those things at church will not get us into Heaven. There are times we have to say no to some of those jobs so we can make time for God. I have had to do this many times. I get so caught up in doing jobs that I don't have time for a relationship with God. Those are the times I have to say no when asked to take on another role or position at church. Maybe we need to ask God to help us with those cluttered times, so our time will be free for Him.

What about the clutter often found in our mouths? The clutter of our mouths, you ask? Yes, too many times we clutter our mouths with things that should never be in there. Like those times our neighbor has told us about another neighbor who did something that wasn't really cool. What is the first thing we do? We can't wait to tell someone else (rumors?!) and then we may just juice it up a bit—you know, to make it a little more interesting. Or when we get angry and those nasty little words come out? Too many times when that happens, you can bet someone (sometimes even a child) is listening and hears us clutter our mouths with those nasty words. Ouch!

Every time we choose to watch a TV show instead of reading the Bible aren't we cluttering our minds? We claim there is no time during the day to read the Bible. We are just too busy. It's amazing to hear people talk about the latest movie they have seen or to hear them talk about what happened on their latest favorite sitcoms. Or the Soap Operas, oh my! You'd think after hearing some people talk that they were related to half the people on the Soaps! When you mention Rachael, Phoebe, Monica, Ross, Chandler, and Joey everyone knows who you are talking about (just in case you *don't*, they are the cast on *Friends*), but how many can tell you who Saul, Philip, Bartholomew, Thomas, or Sarah were? Are we cluttering our minds with things other than the Lord's words, thoughts, and actions?

These are just some of the areas where clutter dwells; I am sure you can look at your own life and find out where your clutter is. We all have it. Ask God to show you your clutter and remove it from your own life. Once you organize and rid yourself of the clutter you can begin to focus on God. Our motto this year should be "cutting the clutter" and, with God's help, we can.

Next time you look at someone's cluttered desk think about the clutter in your own life. I will.

"Do not love this world nor the things it offers you, for when you love the world, you do not have the love of the Father in you. For the world offers only a craving for physical pleasure, a craving for everything we see, and pride in our achievements and possessions. These are not from the Father, but are from this world. And this world is fading away, along with everything that people crave. But anyone who does what pleases God will live forever."

I John 2:15-17

Prayer: Dear Lord, show me the clutter in my life. Lead me to get rid of my clutter and live more fully for you. Thank you for teaching me that clutter is nothing more than worldly desires. Help me as I work toward getting rid of the clutter in my life and grow closer to you. I give you all the honor and glory as I work on my cluttered life. Amen.

Love Is What?

1 John 3:18, John 13:35

Every time someone mentions February, I automatically think of Valentine's Day and love. Love is described in Webster's Dictionary as "a strong affection or liking for someone or something." How many times have you read the definition in the Bible? Or did you know love is described in the Bible? Love is deeper than having affection toward someone or something. Love is not a "February" thing. It's not a "let's share a Valentine and then go back to business as usual on February 15" kind of thing. Love is a way of life.

As described in 1 Corinthians 13:4-7:

"Love is patient and kind. Love is not jealous or boastful or proud or rude. It does not demand its own way. It is not irritable, and it keeps no record of being wronged. It does not rejoice about injustice but rejoices whenever the truth wins out. Love never gives up, never loses faith, is always hopeful, and endures through every circumstance."

In I Corinthians 13, no where does it say we are to love like this just toward our significant other, or our children, or our parents, or those who we choose to love. We are to love every one, in the same way it's described above. Not some, but everyone. In Luke 6:27-28 the Bible tells us, "*But to you who are willing to listen, I say, love your enemies! Do good to those who hate you. Bless those who curse you. Pray for those who hurt you.*" We don't get to choose who we love. We are to love everyone. If we applied this principle to our lives, think how much better our corner of the world would be. Think about how much better all of our world would be.

Taking time and having patience with someone is so much better than always being in a hurry to get there faster or do something quicker.

Being kind and loving at the same time means going the extra mile for people, saying things that will lift their spirits and not drag them down. How many times do we say we love someone and then in the next breath say something that stings, even though it is a "tease"? How many times have we heard someone say something negative and then say, "Oh, I was just teasing"? Were we? Doesn't it still sting?

Love does not envy others. We are not to boast, and we are not to be proud if we say that we love. That means when the Smiths next door get something new (whether it is a new car, new furniture, a faster computer, or something else), we are not to be jealous. We shouldn't try to outdo them. Would it really hurt us to go over and tell them that we are really happy for them? At the same time we are not to boast or be proud. That means if we are the Smiths we are not to "show off" or "brag" about those new things. We are to remain humble and remind ourselves that God gave us the means to buy those things, and He has the means to destroy those things. That's a thought isn't it? God gives and takes away.

This is probably my next favorite part of the scripture about love: "*It is not easily angered and it keeps no record of wrongs.*" Wow! How many times do we get angry with someone and then we store it in the back of our minds, just so we can bring it up again during the next good argument? We are to "forgive and forget," simply said. Do we decide to hold a grudge against someone for half our lives? That only destroys us, not those who we think may have done us wrong.

LOVE IS WHAT?

Throw out all those old records; erase your mind and replace it with love. Love others as you would want to be loved. Jesus has forgiven us of our short comings; shouldn't we do the same with others? Jesus has also wiped our slate clean, and He certainly doesn't hold grudges. Have you ever heard Jesus remind us of something we did long ago? So why should we remind others?

Have you ever thought about love in this manner? Or has love always just been an affectionate thing with you? I challenge each of you to read I Corinthians 13 and start loving as Jesus described it. Make love a way of life, not just a feeling. Learn to love everyone you come into contact with and not just those you choose to love.

> *"Three things will last forever—faith, hope, and love—and the greatest of these is love."*
>
> I Corinthians 13:13

Prayer: Dear Lord, I thank you for loving me. You love me unconditionally. Teach me to love others unconditionally, as well. Help me to remember that love is a lifestyle and not a "Valentine" feeling. Remind me in my daily walk that I am to love those who hurt me, those who try to destroy me, and those who curse me. It is not always easy to love my enemies, but with you living through me I can begin to love others. Thank you for your love. Amen.

Green - A Time to Move Forward

I Corinthians 13:11

Well, March is a month for green and we see a lot of it during this month. St. Patrick's Day is March 17 and you can bet we will see a lot of green then; we also see a lot of shamrocks in March. After looking up some history on St. Patrick's Day, I found out the legend of the shamrock is a true Irish tale, which tells how Patrick used the three-leafed shamrock to explain the Trinity during his ministry. He used it in his sermons to represent how the Father, the Son, and the Holy Spirit could all exist as separate elements of the same body.

For me, green is significant, and I enjoy seeing green in March. After a long winter, it is refreshing to see it. For me, green means growth. Green means a time to move forward. The stoplights are red and green. Green tells us it's time to move forward. We have had a period to stop — now it's time to move on.

Winter is like that for me. Sometimes I stop growing in the winter. Spring and green remind me to move forward. When it gets cold, I just want to stop and stay in. I have to force myself to leave the comfort of my home and go out. When spring comes, I am ready to move out and move forward. I am ready to feel the warmth of the sun and have it shining in my eyes.

That's the way it is with our faith sometimes. We get to the point where we are content with where we are in our faith. We do not want to read the Bible or any other religious book; it's hard for us to go to church, and praying is out of our mind for the present time. We use our down time to do other things or maybe to do nothing. We just stop for a period. Others may try to encourage us, but we just want our down time.

Down time is not really bad; we all need a little. What is bad about down time is the length of time we stay down. We must have a time when we move forward. Something or someone must tell us it's time to move on. When that time comes we must do just that: move on. If we don't move on, then we are stuck and it takes a little more to pull us out. We must realize that if we move forward it helps us look at life in a different, fresher manner. We have more energy to get things done. Our mind is refreshed and ready to take in more knowledge of God's ways and His teachings. When we move forward we are ready to serve God and others. We all have had to move on as human beings — not one of us decided to stay tots all of our life! We moved on to the next stage. When we got to be teenagers we moved on and became adults. Our life is constantly about moving on; so should our faith. Just as we were not satisfied staying children or teenagers, we should not be satisfied with staying where we are in our faith. We had exciting times waiting for us when we moved from tots to teenagers and from teenagers to adults. Those same exciting times can be found each time we move forward in our faith. Just as we were challenged in each step of our lives, we will be challenged as we grow in faith. Our parents were always there encouraging us to move forward, helping us along the way. That is the same way it is with our Father in Heaven, He will be there encouraging us and helping us along the way. We must first be willing to move forward. We must look at the green and know it's time to move forward, to move ahead.

In I Corinthians 13:11 it says, *"When I was a child, I spoke and thought and reasoned as a child. But when I grew up, I put away childish things."* We put those things away and moved on.

When I see green, I get excited knowing it's time to get out and get on the move! I know I am in for some exciting times, as well as some challenging times. I know just as I could trust my parents I can trust my Heavenly Father to help me along the way. Where are you in your faith? Have you stopped at the red light and can't get moving? Have you been stopped for a lot longer than just a season? Do you need someone to come and start pulling you in the forward direction? It's not healthy for us to just stop. We know if we stop challenging our minds at any age we lose the ability to learn new things. It gets harder for us to move forward. This isn't what God wants for us. He wants us, whether we are two or ninety-two, to keep moving forward. This March as you see green, let it remind you that it's time to move forward. It's time to grow, not only in the knowledge of Christ, but also in serving Him. Come along with me this March and let's move forward together.

"This will continue until we all come to such unity in our faith and knowledge of God's Son that we will be mature in the Lord, measuring up to the full and complete standard of Christ."

Ephesians 4:13

Prayer: Dear Lord, thank you for spring and newness of life. As I look at your creation, I see green all around me in the spring. Remind me it's a time to move forward and grow in your knowledge and move toward a deeper relationship with you. I ask you to give me a push if I am stuck at a red light. I thank you for life. Guide me as I move forward in you. Amen.

Making It Personal! Making It Your Story!

Ephesians 6:19-20

Our focus during March and April should be on Easter. We read and reread the story so often that I wonder how often we forget the true meaning. Is it just another "feel good" story in the Bible? Does it become personal for us? Can we feel the pain and the agony Christ went through? What about how Judas felt before and after the betrayal? Or Peter after he denied Christ three times? Can you feel what they felt? Take the time once again to read the story. Read it through one time, and then do something different the second time through (or maybe you need to read it several times through). Pick a character out of the story and put yourself in that character's place. Start with Passion Sunday. Put yourself in the crowd. How would you feel if you saw this man called "Jesus"? Take the time to sit and feel the passion you have for Him. Feel the excitement as He rides in front of you and looks at you. Hear your own voice as you shout, "Hosanna, Hosanna!"

Then put yourself in the Upper Room on that Thursday night. Are you one of the disciples? Are you Judas? Or maybe you are Simon Peter. As one of the disciples, can you feel anger and hostility rise up in you as Jesus begins talking about how one of you will betray Him? As you look at the faces of the other disciples, can you feel distrust and disbelief fill your heart? As your eyes focus on Jesus, are you fearful as you realize that in a few hours He might be taken from you? Do you dwell on the loneliness of losing a mentor?

Maybe you are imagining yourself as Simon Peter as Jesus comes toward you to wash your feet; you look at Him wondering why He is washing your feet when you should be washing His.

"No!" you tell Him. Jesus can't wash your feet. You say you must wash His, but as He replies your heart softens and melts and you allow Jesus to wash your feet. As He takes your feet you feel His love and compassion. Or maybe you are Judas. Maybe you are the one that betrayed Jesus. It seemed so simple a task, but now you feel the hatred the other disciples have for you. You fear for your life. All you want to do is run! After the task is done, all you feel is guilt and shame. Can you feel that guilt and shame? Can you imagine how Judas must have felt?

As you continue reading the Easter story, pick a character and put yourself in Jesus' place. Be in the crowd as they yell for Barabbas' release. Be Barabbas! How would you feel knowing you were going to be freed for a crime you committed, while they were going to hang an innocent man who had done no wrong? Or maybe you are the High Priest, or Pilate or the soldiers who flogged Jesus and twisted together a crown of thorns to place on His head.

Continue until you find yourself at the place called Golgotha. Put yourself in the crowd as they crucify Jesus. Feel the anguish and torment as you see your Savior hanging on the cross. The hopelessness—there is nothing you can do but watch. Feel the compassion as Jesus picks you out of the crowd and looks directly into your eyes. You feel as though you are the only one there. There's no one else, just you and Him. You hear Him as He calls your name, and you know without a doubt He's dying just so you may live and have eternal life. You feel unworthy, but you also feel the "amazing grace"; the grace that "saved a wretch" like you. You want to fall and worship Him. You want to bow and call Him Lord.

Be there on Sunday morning as you go to the empty tomb. You tremble with fear as the angel greets you. The angel tells you Jesus is not there; He has risen just like He said He would! You can't believe it. You can't wait to tell the others. You run as fast as you can. You can feel your

MAKING IT PERSONAL! MAKING IT YOUR STORY

heart beating faster and faster. You are trying to remember everything He told you. It's true! He has gone to prepare a place for you. Someday you will be with Him again, and you are overcome with excitement and joy, knowing it's all true. You want to share this good news with everyone. You want everyone to experience this joy. You yell, you scream, you cry, you laugh, you know. You believe!

Wow! Once you make this story personal it changes things doesn't it? That's the way Jesus wants it. He wants it to be a personal thing. When you experience the emotions, the love, the compassion, and the joy, you can't wait to share those things with everyone you know. You want to "scream it from the mountaintop." You want to go down to the valleys, or the ghettos. You want everyone to know about God's ultimate sacrifice. You know about it, because you've been there. It's your story now, not just a story from the Bible. You have experienced it. You have put yourself there.

This Easter share God's ultimate sacrifice with someone who doesn't know the story or who hasn't made it personal. Bring someone to church during the Holy Week. Help your friend to make the story personal and to realize that as Jesus was hanging on the cross, He was calling out his or her name. He was saying, "I am doing this for you. I am taking away your sins, so you will be made whiter than snow. I am going to go and prepare a place for you."

Or maybe it's you that hasn't made it personal yet. This year make it personal. Make it your story. Then on Easter morning come and sing, "Christ the Lord Has Risen, Hallelujah!" Experience the joy, the love and the peace only Christ can give.

> "And pray for me, too. Ask God to give me the right words so I can boldly explain God's mysterious plan that the Good News is for Jews and Gentiles alike. I am in chains now, still preaching this message as God's ambassador. So pray that I will keep on speaking boldly for him, as I should."
>
> *Ephesians 6:19-20*

L.T. FROG

Prayer: Dear Lord, as I take time to read the Easter story, help me to feel how the people in the Bible felt. Help me to feel the celebration on Palm Sunday, the uncertainty of what was about to take place at the Last Supper, the fear people felt as they saw Jesus' arrest, and their sadness as He was crucified on the cross. Remind me that Jesus did those things so my sins could be washed away and I would be made clean. As I think of the Resurrection let me remember that He has gone to prepare a place for me. Help me to accept God's grace. As I read your Word, help me make it personal; make it my story. Put the desire in my heart to share the Good News with others just as Mary did on that Easter morning. Thank you for dying on the cross so I may live. Amen.

How Could God Reject His Only Son?

Matthew 27:45-46

I hope everyone reading this knows Christ's love and what Easter *really* means. During the months of March and April, we remember Christ's death on the cross and celebrate His resurrection from the tomb into Heaven, where He is sitting with God the Father.

Death is something we don't always want to remember or even think about. In the last few years, death has been a part of my family members' lives. I remember sitting in the hospital for several hours, waiting for the death of my mother-in-law and mother. Several weeks went by as we waited for death to overtake my father-in-law in my own home. Several years ago, my husband and I waited in a hospital in Indianapolis for our son to breathe his last breath. I am very familiar with death and how it affects the lives of families and friends. There have been other close members of my family who I have watched pass away. It's not easy. During the Easter season we will once again pause and remember Jesus Christ being whipped, tortured, and then nailed to a cross. Seeing Him on the cross always saddens me. I feel even worse knowing He did not deserve to die. He was sinless. A sinner was set free in exchange for Christ's death.

There is another aspect I'd like to mention that sometimes

we often overlook. Just as I had to experience the death of loved ones here on Earth, God had to experience and watch the torture of His Son. He had to watch as His Son hung on the cross waiting for Him to take His last breath. The only difference between God and me as we watched our loved ones take their last breaths was that God could do something about His Son's death — I couldn't. Even though Jesus Christ called out to His Father, His Father did nothing. Matthew 27:45-46 says, "At noon, darkness fell across the whole land until three o'clock. At about three o'clock, Jesus called out with a loud voice, 'Eli, Eli, lema sabachthani? . . .'" This means, "My God, my God, why have you abandoned me?"

Can you imagine being God for just a second? Imagine what it must have been like for Him to hear His Son in agony, wanting His Father to save Him. Yet God turned His back on His only Son. Why? Why would God turn away from Him? How could He reject His only Son? Just as it is written in the scriptures,

> "For God loved the world so much that he gave his one and only Son, so that everyone who believes in him will not perish but have eternal life. God sent his Son into the world not to judge the world, but to save the world through him" (John 3:16-17).

So why did God reject His Son at the last minute? So that you and I, if we believe in God the Father, Jesus Christ and the Holy Ghost, may have eternal life. We can live forever! We will not have to experience death, tears, or pain anymore. We can be happy and live in peace forever. Jesus did not deserve dying on the cross, but God allowed Him to die for *our sins* — those things you and I have done wrong. We all have done wrong, and not one of us is without sin. This means Christ died for you. He, who did nothing wrong and never sinned died for you, who has sinned. Pretty awesome thought, isn't it? All we have to do is believe in God and allow God to take over our lives. Give Him complete control.

HOW COULD GOD REJECT HIS ONLY SON?

There is another difference between God and me experiencing death. After three days Jesus Christ was resurrected from His tomb. Mark 16:19 tells us, *"When the Lord Jesus had finished talking with them, he was taken up into heaven and sat down in the place of honor at God's right hand."* God and His only Son were soon reunited. Can you imagine that homecoming? I am sure it was a joyous occasion. I have not experienced that kind of homecoming yet. My loved ones are in Heaven, but I am not there (and don't plan to be for a while). I am still waiting to be reunited with my loved ones. While I can't celebrate a homecoming, I can celebrate in Jesus' resurrection. I can rejoice in the fact that Jesus Christ is alive and is in Heaven with His Father. I can rejoice in the fact that I have a God who was willing to allow His Son to die for me and my sins. As unworthy as I am, He paid the price for me. All I have to do is say yes to His life and give Him control. When Jesus was on the cross I was on His mind! And so were you!

No, it's not easy experiencing the death of a loved one. As we experience death we must remember the resurrection that will take place with our loved ones as they are placed in the grave. They will be resurrected into a new life in Heaven. We must keep our minds focused on the homecoming we will experience and what a joyous occasion it will be.

That's why it is so important for us who are Christians to witness to those who may not know Christ died for them, whether they are family, or friends, or strangers. This Easter, I challenge each of you to share what God has done in your own life. This season, share Christ's death and resurrection with people who don't know Him. Give them the opportunity to share in Christ's resurrection and the hope of a joyous homecoming.

For those who don't know God, I pray this will be the year you will begin to believe! I pray this will be the year you give control of your life over to God. God is waiting for our homecoming with Him. Don't disappoint Him. Believe today!

"There is more than enough room in my Father's home. If this were not so, would I have told you that I am going to prepare a place for you? When everything is ready, I will come and get you, so that you will always be with me where I am."

John 14:2-3

Prayer: Dear Lord, thank you for dying on the cross for my sins. Thank you for preparing a place for me and for the celebration I will experience as I go from this life to the next. When I experience death, let me also remember the resurrection from this life into Heaven. In times of my unbelief, help me to believe and trust in you. Lord, fill me with strength and courage to carry on each day. May each day of my life be a reflection of yours until my homecoming with you. Amen.

In the Merry Month of May

John 19:26

Most people associate the month of May with Mother's Day. It is a time we honor those who gave us life. My mother was the best mom anyone could have, although I know she had her faults as we all do. Because of disease and illness, my mother is no longer with us today.

There is a woman who has tried to fill her shoes. She does not try to take her place, but she tries to fill in for her. Thanks to Lila for being my second mom. She has been there for me when my mom couldn't be. I think that if my mom had to choose anyone to fill in for her, she would have chosen Lila.

Lila has filled in not only because she loves my family and me, but also because she is a Christian. That is what Christianity is all about: loving others as you love yourself. I am sure each of you can think of a special woman who has touched your life as well. Think about her for a minute. What has made her so special? What is it about her that draws you together?

We as Christians are brothers and sisters in Christ. In the Bible Christ calls us His children. In I John 3:1 it says, "See how very much our Father loves us, for he calls us his children, and that is what we are! But the people who belong to this world don't *recognize that we are God's children because they don't know him.*" If we are children of God, then that makes us brothers and sisters in Christ. What we do for our families who were given to us at birth, we should be doing for those around us. Unconditional love—love with no conditions. Love that says, "I love you even though we are not blood related."

As Christ was dying on the cross, even He did not forget about His own mother. He gave His mom to a disciple. For whatever reason, the disciple was given a "fill-in" mom (John 19:26). That is a perfect example of how we are to live our lives. That is a perfect example of a son's love for His mother. I know from Bible studies I have participated in that this disciple took Jesus' mother and treated her as his own, caring for her for the rest of her life.

There may be a mom in your neighborhood that for whatever reason cannot celebrate Mother's Day. There may be Mother's Day Dinners she can't bear to go to. As the Church celebrates Mother's Day during worship service, this woman may have a hard time sitting alone. Take the time to reach out to her unconditionally. Accept Jesus' invitation to accept her as your own. Be that "fill in" Mom for her. Let her know you care.

There are some women who have mothers who are still living, yet they haven't spoken in years, or they are not on the best of terms because of some misunderstanding that happened in the past. Forget what happened, drop the grudge, and reach out to her before it's too late. You don't want to live the rest of your life with regrets. Show your mom how much you care now while she is here.

Most important, love those around you unconditionally. Let them know you love them by adopting them as your brothers and sisters in Christ.

When Christ was on the cross, He didn't pick and choose whom He was going to die for. He died so *all* people may live life eternally. He didn't say to His family, "I do this for you." No, He did it for all of us. He loved each and every one of us, and we must obey Christ and pass that same love on to others.

IN THE MERRY MONTH OF MAY

"Now you are no longer a slave but God's own child. And since you are his child, God has made you his heir."

Galatians 4:7

"If you love only those who love you, why should you get credit for that? Even sinners love those who love them! And if you do good only to those who do good to you, why should you get credit? Even sinners do that much! And if you lend money only to those who can repay you, why should you get credit? Even sinners will lend to other sinners for a full return. Love your enemies! Do good to them. Lend to them without expecting to be repaid. Then your reward from heaven will be very great, and you will truly be acting as children of the Most High, for he is kind to those who are unthankful and wicked. You must be compassionate, just as your Father is compassionate."

Luke 6:32-36

Prayer: Dear Lord, thank you for my mother. I give you praise for those women who have reached out to me in love. I am so blessed to have been adopted into your family. As I look to my left and right, I see my brothers and sisters in Christ. Give me the desire to reach out in love to them and to treat them as if they really are my brothers and sisters. Help me to seek out those women who have lost their mothers or those who have lost their children. Help me as I build new relationships with those close to me. I ask that you, O Lord, pour out your blessings on your child. In turn, I pray that you will be blessed by my thoughts and actions as I learn to live for you more fully each day. All these things I pray, Amen.

Father Knows Best

Hebrews 12:6-9

In June, we celebrate Father's Day, and we will begin to reflect on our fathers. I was thinking about fathers the other day; they are special to each of us. Have we really thought about what it takes to be a "really good" father? Let's reflect for a few minutes.

Fathers are supposed to be just that: a father, not our best friend. Because they are supposed to be fathers we are not happy with them 100 percent of the time. If a father is a good one, he will not give us everything we want. He knows some things are okay for us to have, and he will provide for us certain things we want but don't always need. For instance, we don't need to have a pet. A lot of times we talk our dad into getting us a pet. (He often thinks this may teach us responsibility, but often times we love the pet and someone else gets stuck taking care of it.) There are times candy is not needed, but we can often get our dad to purchase a candy bar for us (especially if mom isn't around).

I can remember having slumber parties when I was younger. My mom wasn't always a big fan of them (maybe because she got stuck watching us while Dad slept), so when I wanted a slumber party, Dad was always there to say, "Yes, of course." The slumber party wasn't needed, but it was an okay thing.

If fathers spoil us and give us everything we need, then we will always want and want and want. We will no longer wait to see what the answer may be; we will just expect that it will be given to us. We will become ungrateful for the things we get and our dads will become unappreciated — not a healthy thing for us or for him. We will soon become a demanding person, always wanting more and more.

Another area Dad is not always popular with us is in giving us advice. Sometimes we get advice from Dad even when we don't ask for it. There are times we would just like for our fathers to keep their noses out of our business, yet, if he loved us and cared for us he would be concerned for us and watch what we do. Our business will be his business. An example would be right after we have first learned to drive and we are out on our own; someone tells Dad we were caught speeding. Dad calls us in and tells us it is not best to speed. Speed can cause problems if we are not careful. We could lose control of the car, have an accident, and kill ourselves or whoever is with us. So he advises us to slow down. We are a better driver than he thinks. We know what is best for us. So, we continue driving fast until we get a ticket, have an accident or Dad catches us and ground us.

Or maybe we are hanging out with the wrong crowd. Dad sets us down and tells us the consequences of hanging out with the wrong crowd. Drinking, drugs, or even criminal acts could become a part of our lives. Maybe, he suggests, we want to hang out with a different crowd. We see nothing wrong with our friends. Dads have often been down those same roads and know what lies ahead of us. They are just trying to protect us and keep us from getting into trouble later. If Dad would just mind his own business, life would be better, or so we think.

Then, of course, there is the punishment factor. If Dad is going to be a good one, he will eventually have to discipline us. We have done wrong and Dad finds out about it. He could let it go, and we could get by with it. Eventually if we continue down the wrong road things could get a whole lot worse. Instead of Dad punishing us the next time, it could be the police. It would be better for all of us if Dad would take the time to punish us and set us straight. Of course we will hear, "This hurts me worse than it does you, but you need it. I am doing this for your own good. Trust me." *Yeah right*, you think.

Dad also will not let us do everything we want to do. Dad knows that when we are young, if we put our hand on the stove it's going to burn, so he stops us. We decide we want to tour the world instead of going to college. Dad knows this isn't a good thing, so he won't let us; instead, he forces us to get a job or go to college.

After we have grown up, we think our dad is the smartest, best and greatest dad anyone could have. He hasn't changed, we have matured. We now know dad was right in not letting us have everything or giving us everything or letting us do everything. His advice was pretty sensible. We are now sensible and responsible people with kids of our own to discipline, just like our dad did.

As Christians, we often go through the same thoughts with our Heavenly Father as we are maturing in our faith. How many times have we gone to our Heavenly Father and asked Him to give us something we really didn't need, but just wanted? You know, like the new car? Mine is okay, but if I could just have a newer car, the guys would really like me better, or I would be respected more. If I could just have that promotion, I could provide a better home for my family. If I could just get a raise, I would be able to do more for my family. I would definitely give more to the church (then we suddenly forget that promise). We keep asking and asking. Then we get upset because God hasn't always come through for us. It's like He has deaf ears. Why can't you just give me a few things? Well, maybe He knows what is best for us. What a thought!

We are out one night having fun with our friends, then suddenly God decides to give us advice. "You know you shouldn't be here" or "You know what can happen if you don't quit drinking now" or "Do you really think you need to be telling those kinds of jokes?" We're sitting there with our friends and God decides to advise us on what we should and shouldn't be doing. We're getting more uncomfortable the longer we sit there. If He'd just mind His own business and quit telling me what to do, we think. When I want to know what to do I'll ask Him! We get so uncomfortable that we finally have to leave the scene. God has ruined another good evening.

We decide we want to move to another state. You ask God to open doors so that circumstances will work out for us, but doors close on us. We can't get the right doors to open, and we find that we are stuck where we are. We try our luck at something else and that fails, too. It seems God won't let us do anything.

Does God punish us? This is a big question. Everyone has an opinion on it. My answer is found the Bible. In the Bible it says:

> *"For the Lord disciplines those he loves, and he punishes each one he accepts as his child. As you endure this divine discipline, remember that God is treating you as his own children. Who ever heard of a child who is never disciplined by its father? If God doesn't discipline you as he does all of his children, it means that you are illegitimate and are not really his children at all. Since we respected our earthly fathers who disciplined us, shouldn't we submit even more to the discipline of the Father of our spirits, and live forever?" (Hebrews 12:6-9).*

So, just as our earthly father disciplines us, so does our Heavenly Father. When our fathers discipline us we know it is for our own good and to teach us important lessons. We must stop and look at the lesson God is teaching us and grow from it. We must not hold grudges; we just need to learn from it and move on.

There is one big difference between our Heavenly Father and our earthly fathers. There are times we just can't get along with our earthly fathers and we go our separate ways. Once in a while, we'd like to be able to go back and begin a relationship with the one we've lost. Sometimes, it works out and sometimes it doesn't. With our Heavenly Father, we can always be assured that God is waiting for us with wide open arms. He will never reject us. No matter what we have said or done, or how we have acted, He will be there waiting. All we have to do is take the first step. Remember the Prodigal Son? Remember how he was received by his father? It's the same way with God. He will rejoice and be happy we have come back to Him. He will love us even when our fathers here on Earth have quit loving us. When our fathers on Earth see failure, our Heavenly Father sees possibilities in us. When there is no one to turn to, we can always turn to God. He will be waiting for us.

As we grow in our faith and we mature, we too will realize God was right all along. He is the smartest dad we could have. He is the best. All His advice is right on the money. All the things He allows us to do were right and all those times He shuts the door, He knows what He is doing. When we celebrate Father's Day, take a minute to think about the relationship you have with your Heavenly Father. Then take another minute to thank Him for all He has done for you, for all the unwanted advice, and for shutting those doors. Let Him know you realize how wonderful He really is and you are very thankful for a Father like Him.

> *"And have you forgotten the encouraging words God spoke to you as his children? He said, 'My child, don't make light of the Lord's discipline, and don't give up when he corrects you . . . .'"*
>
> *Hebrews 12:5*

Prayer: I give you thanks, O Lord, for my father. Often times I don't respect my father as I should. I think he is too harsh and interfering. Yet, most of the time he knows what is best for me. I ask that you would be with my father; give him wisdom and knowledge in your ways. Help my father to seek you as his role model. Thank you also for being a perfect parent. I am so blessed to be called your child. May I in turn be a blessing to you as I strive to live more fully for you each day. I ask all these things in your name. Amen.

F.R.O.G. - Fully Rely On God

Philippians 3:3, Psalm 56:3-4

On July 20, 2001, I had my first major surgery. I had never been in the hospital for any reason except to have my children. I always told my husband I would be a basket case if I ever had to have surgery. I hate needles, and I am not fond of pain. It took several months to get the courage to have surgery. Once I had it scheduled, I had to wait some six weeks. All that time to think and fret! Well, I didn't think about it, and I didn't fret. I was too busy working ahead to keep things done.

The Sunday before I was to go to surgery, my Pastor anointed me with oil, and several people prayed with me. I felt peace about the whole situation. That week I had several appointments to keep. Several people knew I was having surgery and said they would pray for me (especially when they found out I was a rookie). I have Christian e-mail buddies who knew of my upcoming surgery, and they all offered to pray for me that day.

The big day came. I was sure I would be scared and very nervous. As we were preparing to leave home, I heard about an accident that had become a traffic jam on the road that would lead me to the hospital. Instead of fretting about the surgery, I now had to fret about getting there on time. Upon arriving at the hospital, my nerves began to jump around. Once I got to the surgical floor, all the nurses treated me like royalty. As I lay in my bed waiting for things to start happening, I was getting a little more nervous. On TV they have a channel that is supposed to reduce stress and tension. I turned it on. What I saw was God's beautiful creation. There were scenes of mountains, oceans, wildlife, and many other things. I could sense God's presence envelope me. I also realized as I lay there that there was nothing to fear. I had so many Christian friends praying for me. I also remembered the number of frogs I have collected and their true meaning. All I had to do was *fully rely on God* to take care of me. A peace came over me, and I realized I was going to be okay. Even if something unusual happened and I didn't make it, I still would be okay because I would wake up in heaven.

As I woke up in recovery I was ecstatic! Surgery was over, and I had made it. I asked the nurse taking care of me two questions and then it was lights out again. I could rest in peace knowing it was all over for me.

Several years have passed since my first surgery. I am still amazed that I did not freak out. I know why I didn't. I did what I have told so many people and my children to do on several occasions. Something so simple, it sounds too easy: I had people pray for the situation I was going through, and then I put my faith and trust in God and forgot about the situation. I allowed God to envelope me with His love through so many prayers from family and friends. I fully relied on God to take care of the situation. I placed my life in His hands and went on.

I hope I never need to have another surgery, but if I do I know it will be okay. I am no longer terrified of needles, IVs, shots, and pain. I have even donated blood at blood drives, which is something I have always wanted to do but never have had the nerve. Now I go in like an old pro. It's no big deal when you know you are doing something to help someone else.

The next time you are terrified of something you have to go through or of something you are now going through, remember to call someone: a friend, your pastor. Include your church so they can pray for you. Call and ask as many friends as you can to pray for you, then buy a frog to keep near you. Every time you look at the frog remember to *fully rely on God*, and then do just that. Put your faith and trust in Him. You will receive strength, courage, power, and peace to see you through. It is a most wonderful feeling. The peace is like something you have never experienced before. It is the kind of peace that passes all understanding. It's the kind of peace that gives you strength and courage to get through what is ahead of you. Now, go schedule that surgery or do that task that you haven't wanted to do. Before you do, ask others to pray for you as you go do what you need to do. Then sit back and remember to *fully rely on God!*

"But when I am afraid, I will put my trust in you. I praise God for what he has promised. I trust in God, so why should I be afraid? What can mere mortals do to me?"

Psalm 56:3-4

Prayer: Thank you, Father, for not leaving me or forsaking me in my time of need. I give you praise for those people you send to help me in my time of need. I ask that you bless those prayer warriors who take the time to remember me and lift me up in prayer. As I put my trust in you, help me to move beyond that trust and learn to fully rely on you to meet my needs. I honor you and give you praise and glory for all you are doing in my life. Amen.

A Summer of Blessings

Matthew 5:16, Mark 16:15-16

In August, children are returning to school. People begin to get into a routine again as fall approaches. We begin to slow down and spend less time on the road and vacationing. We begin to make plans for the holidays and begin to settle in for winter. Fall is a slow-down time period, which I think we all need.

As I reflect on a particular summer several things come to mind. The first thing is an event that took place at the county fair. My family and I traveled to Delaware County for the rodeo. One of the things that impressed me the most took place before the rodeo. A few minutes before it started, the announcer said it was time for the Cowboys' Prayertime. I didn't pay too much attention. Then all of a sudden I looked down on the field and there were twenty or thirty men dressed as cowboys down on their knees, heads bowed and in prayer. Wow! What a witness to the several hundred people who attended and watched. Here were these rough and tough men who knew their strength and trust came from God. It gave me cold chills and brought tears to my eyes as I watched these men pray for each other, for themselves, and for their safety. It made me stop and offer a prayer of thanks for their witness. As the group of cowboys dismissed, one or two of them lingered in prayer a little longer. It was an awesome sight. It made me feel proud once again to be called a Christian. We are all part of the family of God, and these were my brothers in Christ.

Later during the summer, my family and I had the opportunity to vacation in Florida. We took Johnny, my son-in-law's father, and Johnny had never met a stranger. Johnny had a stroke several years ago and is in a wheel chair. One evening, one of the friends Johnny met came over and sat around the table at our campground. He and his wife were Christians. We spent the next few minutes sharing our faith with each other. We had never met before, yet after he left it seemed as if he had been a friend for life. He didn't know us, but he shared with us his faith and love for Christ. He was another wonderful witness to what Christ is doing in people's lives.

When I came home, I had an appointment at the doctor's office. I went in as usual, not expecting to share my faith with anyone. As I was called back to the office, the nurse and I started talking as she took my vitals and gathered some information. Before long we had engaged in a conversation about our faith. I shared with her the book I was reading and suggested she get it and read it. She and I shared our love for Christ with each other and the things He was doing in our lives. I had received yet another opportunity to witness and share my faith with others.

I was also blessed by the actions of other people that particular summer, as I watched them share their faith in Christ and their love for one another. The church I was attending was getting ready to welcome a new pastor. The parsonage needed some work done on it before his arrival. I watched as so many people dug their heels in and worked on the parsonage. A couple in our church gave up many hours and worked really hard on the home, getting it ready for the new pastor and his wife. There were many others who gave up free time or took time away from something else to work on the parsonage. They did it all for a perfect stranger. Why? It was because each one of these people was totally committed to Christ and to sharing their faith and love with one another. What a witness it was to see them work together to help provide a beautiful home

A SUMMER OF BLESSINGS

for the pastor. The wife of the couple who worked on the parsonage had once lived in that home as a youth; her dad had been a pastor there. She related how this house had been her mom's favorite parsonage. Susie's mother passed away while she was working on this house. What a blessing and how healing it must have been for Susie to work on her mother's favorite parsonage. Maybe this was God's way of helping Susie cope with the death of her mother.

One night we had a "Spaghetti, Talent/No-Talent Show" at our church. This was another example of God's love shining through people. We laughed, we shared our faith, and we loved. We loved not only each other, but we also shared our love with outsiders and those who were new to our church.

Finally, there was another lady who witnessed her faith with me that summer. My father celebrated his eightieth birthday and we had an open house. We asked that no gifts be brought. A friend brought in this huge box, and we all wondered what it could be. She took me over to the box before she left and shared with me what was inside: It was several individual containers of frozen homemade vegetable and chili soup for my dad to eat that winter. She had given up her time and made homemade meals for my dad. Now, I know most of us don't have a lot of extra time. This lady works three afternoons each week. She also has health problems, yet she took the time to do something for someone else. Why? She, too, is a Christian lady and what better way to share Christ's love than by sacrificing her time to help someone else out. Wow!

I could give you several more examples of people either sharing their faith with me or me receiving a blessing as I watched others share their faith. It was truly a summer filled with God allowing me to see He is still in control and, yes, He is still working in people's lives. We sing a song that has come to my mind. The song, "They'll Know We Are Christians by Our Love", is a perfect example of what I saw one summer. By sharing our love with others, people <u>will</u> know we are Christians. It says in John 13:35, "*Your love for one another will prove to the world that you are my disciples.*" That particular summer it seemed to me that people were sharing their faith more and were opening up more about what God was doing in their lives. How will others know of Christ's love if we never share it? When we share our faith with one another, whether through our actions or words, it makes us stronger. It makes our faith more real. I have heard this phrase repeated over and over and it is worth repeating one more time: We may be the only minister or pastor some people ever meet. If God gives us that opportunity and we don't take it, don't you think He will hold us accountable? If we are ashamed of sharing His message and love with others, He will be ashamed of us and say He never knew us. Each year as September 11 approaches, people look for something to put their faith and trust in. Let us be there and be ready to share our love and faith with them. Let us witness in deeds, actions, or words to others so they may know we are Christians. Let others see the love we have for Christ in our everyday life and let's be willing to share that love with everyone.

> "I tell you the truth, everyone who acknowledges me publicly here on earth, the Son of Man will also acknowledge in the presence of God's angels. But anyone who denies me here on earth will be denied before God's angels."
>
> Luke 12:8-9

Prayer: Dear Lord thank you for those who choose to serve you. I give you thanks, O Lord, for those who willingly share their faith with others. Bless those who serve you. May I share my faith with those who are not aware of your love for them. Make me aware of those around me who need to know you in a personal way. Help me as I reach out to them. Give me wisdom and knowledge as I seek to do your will. I ask all these things in thy name. Amen.

School Days

Matthew 19:13

In September of 1999, another school year had begun. I was having mixed emotions that year. That would be the last year I would be sending students to school. Though this was our last year, for many others this year would be no different. They would continue sending children and grandchildren to school. Some would be sending children to school for the very first time. This may have caused some people to have some mixed emotions, as well.

As I reflected back on the years that my daughters attended school, I was reminded how fast the time passed. It seemed as if only yesterday they were beginning; now, they were finishing.

Do I have advice for you first time parents? The most important thing I did for my kids was I made sure every morning to walk to the door with them, wait with them for the bus, and then give them a hug and a kiss. I told them to have a good day, as well. The next thing I did was equally important to both the girls and me. As they walked to the bus, I prayed. I prayed for their safety, for their mind to be opened up to the information the teachers would share with them, and I prayed they and their schoolmates would get along with each other. Some of the best times we had were those mornings. We would talk, laugh, and yes, even disagree about things sometimes.

I never feared for my children because I knew each morning I placed them in God's hand, and no matter what happened He would take care of them. It is never too late to start praying daily for your children, grandchildren, or the neighborhood children.

The other advice I have for each of you is to take time for your kids because it will fly by. I don't have any regrets — I always participated in my children's activities. I did nine years of band contests. Can you imagine how much music I heard? How many band members' faces I must have seen! I did get more than my share! Wow! There were times I was really tired and didn't want to go, but once I got there and saw the look on my child's face, I knew I had made the right decision.

Over the years, I have been to several activities with our daughters. One of the things I noticed is my kids always seemed to have a bunch of kids hanging around them. I would ask the kids if their parents were there. It surprised me to hear so many of the kids say mom or dad had not shown up. Therefore, we were "adopted" a lot. To some of the kids, I believe their absent parents sent a message that maybe mom and dad weren't really interested in what they were doing or maybe they weren't on the top of mom and dad's priority list. Is that the kind of message we want to send to our kids? There is nothing so important to us, as parents, that we can't take time out for our children. We would never think about neglecting our kids as babies. That would be child abuse. Our children, when they were babies, were our top priorities. We took time to feed them, change their diapers, rock them, and all the other things that go with babies. So, why do we sometimes neglect them as children or teens? Why do we not continue making them our top priorities?

Participating in your children's lives will not only benefit them: You, too, will reap many benefits. The joys I have received over the years, hearing many kids call me their "adopted mom," is beyond measure. I never had to worry about where my kids were; they were usually home with lots of other kids hanging around. The laughter, the loud music, and the fun times will be something we will always remember and cherish. There were a lot of times I never knew how many would be there for supper or how many were sleeping over. This also gave me the opportunity to witness to kids who may never have had the chance to hear God's word or see God's plan in action. All the kids who slept over on Saturday night knew they would be attending church the next day with us. That was a rule. I may have been the only minister these kids would ever see.

I thank God every day for the opportunity I have had as a parent. It has been a joy to both my husband and me. Whether you realize it or not, you are molding your child's life. How you treat your children will be how your children treat your grandchildren.

Take time to pray for your children daily and take the time to go to their activities with them. If each parent begins to pray for their student and school, if each parent begins to take an interest in their kids and their activities, you will begin to see a big change in our society and in our schools.

As our children leave school we must continue to pray for those students and teachers still involved in our school system. Our students today will become tomorrow's leaders. It is only through our prayers and our interest in them that they will become the best they can be.

"But if you refuse to serve the Lord, then choose today whom you will serve. . .But as for me and my family, we will serve the Lord."

Joshua 24:15

"Fathers, do not provoke your children to anger by the way you treat them. Rather, bring them up with the discipline and instruction that comes from the Lord."

Ephesians 6:4

L.T. FROG

Prayer: Dear Lord, thank you for blessing me with children and grandchildren. Give me direction and wisdom as I raise these children. It is not always easy in times like these; with the world screaming at them, I am not always heard. Give my children knowledge, protect them from evil, and keep them safe. Teach me as a parent and grandparent to be patient, and help me to listen to them and love them when it sometimes seems hard. I give you thanks for their lives and their love. Help me, as a parent, to be worthy of their love. All these things I ask in thy name. Amen.

Campfires and Faith

Matthew 5:14-16

My husband and I love to camp. We enjoy seeing new places and have met a lot of wonderful people. One night, we were sitting around the campfire when God spoke to me. As I looked at the fire, I realized the only way the fire keeps burning is if my husband puts more wood on it. When he stops putting wood on the fire, it eventually burns down. When he adds more wood, it begins to burn and we can see the flames once again. Pretty simple concept, huh?

    I began to think about faith and the Christian walk and how it relates to fire. When we first become Christians, we are like the fire with flames shooting up. We are excited and we want to share with everyone. We are on fire for the Lord! Sometimes it is hard to contain us; we want to go in a million different directions. We have lots of thoughts and ideas to share with others. We want them to know about our love for Christ and His love for us. We are eager to read our Bibles, we want to pray, we want to witness, and we go on and on. As time passes, we begin to slow down. If we are not careful, we begin to burn out. We forget one day to read the Bible, or we forget to say our prayers. Or maybe we have a chance to share our witness and don't. Our fire begins to slowly burn down.

Then one day, we suddenly realize our fire for the Lord is now just an ember. How did it get that way? What happened? How do we once again get on fire for the Lord?

Sometimes we have to stoke the fire and then begin to add wood to the fire. How do we do that in our Christian walk? We do that by learning to set priorities. We need to look to see what has prevented us from taking the time to read our Bible or pray. We have to figure out what is more important in our lives. Yes, families are important, but it is more important to stop and pray and read the Bible. We must put God first in our lives and our families second. I know this is a hard task to do. At one time, I realized God was second and my family was first. My fire was beginning to burn down. If we don't put God first, and if we allow our families to run over us and constantly are taking time for them (and not for ourselves), then we will run out of steam. We become a machine doing things for them and no longer living for Christ. We do things automatically. We have to let our families know what is important in our lives. They need to know they are important, but they also need to realize God is first in our lives. They need to realize that if we take the time to read the Bible and pray it will help us be better parents. Having God on our team, we will be better equipped to handle the everyday happenings. If your family sees you praying and reading your Bible, what better witness can you be for them? They will learn from you how to let God be first in their lives. They will realize how you and God are handling things. What a great impression to leave on your children or grandchildren.

Another way to revive a fire is to add wood to it. How do you revive your faith? Once a year or every couple of years, I think we need to look at attending a retreat; a time to get away from family. A time to sing praises, to share with others, to study His Word; a time to reflect and then a time to renew your own faith. We need a time to revive that fire.

There are several retreats that are available. Ask your pastor or church secretary if they know of one. If one is not available, then get some of your peers together and go away and have your own retreat. Go somewhere that you can take some music to sing along with, take your Bibles to study from and then just be willing to open up to share with others. Nothing is more healing or refreshing than to hear from others how God is working in their lives. You will come back refreshed, and your fires will be burning once again.

Instead of letting your fire burn down to an ember, take time every day to maintain your fire. Add a little wood every day by reading your Bible, taking time to pray for others, and listening to God. Going to church is an excellent way to keep those fires burning, but not just one morning a week. We need that midweek service or that Bible study to help us keep the fires burning. Here is an idea: how about having a prayer partner to keep us accountable and to help us through the rough times and even to share the good times with?

As I sit and watch my husband while we camp, I see that he is constantly keeping the fire burning. He is poking, adding wood, or just keeping an eye out for when it begins to die down. That is the way it should be with our faith. We should be constantly working on our faith. We need to maintain our faith daily. We should be busy keeping our faith on fire for the Lord. We should never let our faith become just an ember. It says in Matthew 5:14-16:

> *"You are the light of the world—like a city on a hilltop that cannot be hidden. No one lights a lamp and then puts it under a basket. Instead, a lamp is placed on a stand, where it gives light to everyone in the house. In the same way, let your good deeds shine out for all to see, so that everyone will praise your heavenly Father."*

If our fire for the Lord is nothing but embers, how will others see our light? If you get a chance this fall to sit around a campfire, reflect on your own fire. How are you doing at burning? Are you just an ember, or are you on fire for the Lord, or are you just slowly burning out? If you are burning out, start poking at the fire and begin adding wood. Don't be just an ember.

L.T. FROG

"But those who trust in the Lord will find new strength. They will soar high on wings like eagles. They will run and not grow weary. They will walk and not faint."

Isaiah 40:31

"Create in me a clean heart, O God. Renew a loyal spirit within me."

Psalm 51:10

Prayer: Dear Lord, as I study your Word, pray, and go to church, it is my desire to keep the fire burning. It is hard sometimes to keep the fire from burning out. You have given me hope. I know if I trust you, you will renew my strength and my fire once again will burn brightly. I want to soar like an eagle, I want to run and not grow weary, but it is only with your strength that I can do that. Help me not to trust in my own strength, but in yours. I thank you for your love, your grace, and your mercy. I give you all the honor and glory as I once again renew my faith in you. Thank you also for creating in me a clean heart and renewing my spirit. All these things I ask in your name. Amen.

A Beautiful Weed

Acts 9

I love fall. It is one of my favorite seasons. One autumn day, I had just come back from a walk to the post office in town. There was a small breeze; just enough to kick up the leaves that had already fallen to the ground. As I looked at the leaves, I noticed that they were a pretty golden color. Even though it was unusually warm for October, the air felt like fall. The colors this time of the year are just magnificent.

I had just started walking on a regular basis. I lived out in the country so I walked out my drive and down the gravel road. My routine was to go a half-mile and then turn onto a paved road. Since we lived out in the country we didn't have much traffic. The wild flowers were in bloom and were beautiful. There were some pretty purple flowers and yellow flowers that I am sure were nothing more than weeds of some kind. They were just beautiful and had caught my eye. Later in the day, I told my daughter as she was driving me to work that I might just have to stop and pick some of those flowers and make a bouquet. I know some people might think I'm a nut — why would I want to make a bouquet out of weeds? Why not go to the florist and choose some beautiful flowers, like roses, to make a bouquet? The rose is a beautiful flower, I will agree with you. To me, though, the flowers out in the fields and alongside roads remind me of the people Jesus ministered to.

Jesus spent His time in the ministry teaching the common people, the people on the streets. Some of these people were even thought of as weeds. You know the kind of people that some folks would like to see disappear. They were those who suffered from diseases like leprosy, or were blind, or deaf, or like the man who had the demons inside of him. That's the kind of people Jesus ministered to. In Matthew 9:12 it says, *"When Jesus heard this, he said, 'Healthy people don't need a doctor—sick people do.'"*

Once Jesus healed the people from their diseases, many of them were grateful and praised Him. Once they were cured or healed they would go and share their good news with neighbors, friends, and family. Jesus healed a man with leprosy. After healing him Jesus warned him not to tell anyone. In Mark 1:45 it says, *"But the man went and spread the word, proclaiming to everyone what had happened. . . ."* Again in Mark, Jesus healed a demon possessed man. In Mark 5:20, it says, *"So the man started off to visit the Ten Towns of that region and began to proclaim the great things Jesus had done for him; and everyone was amazed at what he told them."* Once people were healed, they began to share the good news with others. Weeds often spread quickly and often take up a lot of ground. Just like the weeds, the stories of healing spread everywhere.

There is another aspect to this we must think about. What is a weed in one man's eyes is a rose in another's eyes. Like the old saying goes, "one man's trash is another man's treasure." I did make a bouquet of what my kids called weeds. It was beautiful, or so I thought. The kids made fun of it. I would comment about my beautiful fall bouquet and the kids would laugh and say, "Mom it is just a bunch of weeds." I would reply, "Yes, but to me they are beautiful weeds." The bouquet reminded me of my life. Once I was a weed, but God took my life and made it into a beautiful bouquet, something I was proud of. We are told several times in the Bible that we are not to judge one another. Luke 6:37 says,

A BEAUTIFUL WEED

"Do not judge others, and you will not be judged. Do not condemn others, or it will all come back against you. Forgive others, and you will be forgiven." As we look at those people who we consider weeds, God sees them as possibilities waiting to happen. One day those weeds may turn into a beautiful flower for all to see. We may stand and look at that beautiful weed in awe of what God has done in his or her life. Do you know of someone who you had considered a weed that was just taking up space, but through God's grace and mercy was turned into a beautiful flower? There are several examples in the Bible. Moses murdered someone, yet God turned him into a beautiful flower at which we all marvel. David committed adultery and had someone murdered, yet he is a significant person in the Bible. The most prominent weed in the Bible was Paul. How many Christians did Paul murder? Yet God placed His hand on Paul. Paul's life reflects God's love, mercy, and grace. He was a beautiful weed.

Remember that before Christ began working in each of us, we were nothing more than a weed. When we allowed God to work in us and make changes in us we became a beautiful flower. As you drive by fields, stop and look at the beautiful "weeds" popping up. Think about your own life: Has it gone from just a weed to a beautiful flower? How would you want others to see you?

> *"Do not judge others, and you will not be judged. Do not condemn others, or it will all come back against you. Forgive others, and you will be forgiven."*
>
> *Luke 6:37*

> *"When Jesus heard this, he told them, 'Healthy people don't need a doctor—sick people do. I have come to call not those who think they are righteous, but those who know they are sinners.'"*
>
> *Mark 2:17*

L.T. FROG

Prayer: Dear Lord, as I pass fields where weeds abound, let me reflect on my own life and remember I once was a weed, too. Thank you for taking my life and making me into a beautiful flower. Help me not to pass judgment on those I think are weeds. Let me remember that you see them as possibilities. I give you praise for what you are doing in my life. Let my life reflect your love and beauty. I ask all these things in thy name. Amen.

What Costume Are You Wearing?

Psalm 139

By October each year I am asking myself, where has the time gone? Before you know it, the holidays will be here. One of the holidays that kids like to celebrate will take place at the end of this month. We all know it as Halloween. I know when my kids were younger we went to the store and looked for hours for a costume. They always had a hard time deciding who they wanted to be. We would only let them choose characters that we thought were okay. For instance, cartoon characters, princesses, etc. I am not here to give you my opinion on whether Christians should or should not celebrate Halloween. That is between you and God.

What I am going to do is look at the costumes themselves. Costumes are designed for the purpose of wearing them and allowing ourselves to be the person or thing the costume portrays. For example, a few years ago all the boys wanted to be Ninja Turtles or some other super-power hero. Why? They could pretend for one night they were a superhero and had all that power given to them. We all know they were the same children, even with the costumes on. They didn't have power, and they weren't superheroes.

Most of us agree that as adults, we are too old to dress up in costumes and go trick-or-treating. Many of us are fooling ourselves. We may not go out and purchase a costume and we may not go trick-or-treating, but in reality too many of us wear costumes daily and we try to trick others into believing we are something we aren't.

There are people who put on the costume of a successful person. They want to trick you into believing they are very successful and life is just grand. They may have all the appearances of a successful person: a nice car, a beautiful home, a good job; everything they have appears as if they are a success. Once the costume is taken off, are they really successful? Does all that success make them happy? What about all the debt they have accumulated just to trick others into thinking they are successful? Is their success based on a relationship with Christ or is it based on worldly success?

There is the costume of being at peace with everything and everybody. You ask them how things are going and they are the first ones to say everything is fine when, in reality, their lives are in shambles. You see them smile and pretend that life is pleasant all the time. They may have all kinds of health issues, family problems, or they themselves are experiencing depression, yet to the world everything is fine. They put on their costume and pretend.

Another costume adults, like children, wear is that of the superhero. They put this costume on and they become the hero. They truly believe they have the power to do anything, be anybody, and get by with anything. These people think they don't need God, and they can do it themselves. They have all the power and strength, and God is a waste of their time. They are in control of their circumstances and no one is going to tell them any different.

These are just a few costumes we all put on from time to time. You have done it and so have I. The question is what kind of costume are you wearing now? Who are you trying to trick people into believing you are?

At church on Sunday morning, you may see these and many other costumes coming into church. People can't allow anyone in church to see who they really are. Yet, that is when we need to shed our costumes and come just as we are. Well, I have news for you. We may try to trick our family and friends. We can wear all kinds of costumes and try to hide

WHAT COSTUME ARE YOU WEARING?

our real identity. We may think no one will ever see the real us. In Psalm 139:1 it says, *"O Lord, you have examined my heart and know everything about me."* God knows everything there is to know about us. We cannot hide anything from Him. We cannot hide our deepest feelings, we can't hide our words, and we can't hide our thoughts from Him: nothing.

Even with the costume on, you are still you. You can deceive man into thinking you are someone else, but you can't deceive God. Underneath that costume, God knows you. He knows your weaknesses and He knows your strengths. He knows what you can and can't do. He knows whom you will obey—Satan or God.

A few days ago on TV, I saw some people who had gone in for a complete makeover. Some of them had nose jobs, plates put in their chins, tummy tucks, and all other sorts of things. It really bothered me because God made them who they were. Instead of appreciating God's creation, they felt doctors could do a better job, so they allowed doctors to mess with God's creation. That in itself is disappointing to me, but you know what? Nothing has changed. Yes, their looks have changed, but they are still themselves even after all the operations. Deep down inside they are still the same people they were before. They may put on a costume to try and deceive people into thinking they are different, but God knows better. There is nothing we can do that God doesn't know about. There is no costume that will hide who we are from God.

The sad part of this is far too many people fail to realize God loves them for who they are. They don't have to put on a costume for God to love them. In Romans 8:35 it reads, *"Can anything ever separate us from Christ's love? . . ."* In 8:38 it goes on to say:

> *"And I am convinced that nothing can ever separate us from God's love. Neither death nor life, neither angels nor demons, neither our fears for today nor our worries about tomorrow—not even the powers of hell can separate us from God's love."*

In simple terms, that means that nothing the doctor does, no costume, *nothing* can separate us from the love God has for us. He will love us no matter what we are like. All we have to do is be willing to take off our costume, go to Him, and allow Him to love us for who we really are; not what we think we are or who we want to be.

We must also realize we can have better relationships with our family and friends if they are allowed to see the real us and not hide behind some costume. Unless they, too, are hiding behind some costume, they will love us for who we really are. They won't care about our looks, actions, or what we have done in the past.

Are you ready to take off your costume? Are you ready to quit tricking people into thinking you are something you aren't? Once you have removed your costume and quit playing the tricking game, your load will be a lot lighter.

For Halloween this year, let's leave the costumes and the trick-or-treating to the kids and let's get real with ourselves, family, friends, and God. Remember: God loves you for you; not for what you think you ought to be or what you think He wants you to be!

"Can anything ever separate us from Christ's love? Does it mean he no longer loves us if we have trouble or calamity, or are persecuted, or hungry, or destitute, or in danger, or threatened with death?"

Romans 8:35

Prayer: Lord, I want to take my costume off, but I am afraid. I am afraid people won't like me for who I really am. I am afraid people will see my brokenness and turn the other way. When I wear my costume I can become who I want to be. I can pretend to be somebody I am not. You know me, Lord, inside and out. I can trick people, but I can't trick you. Help me as I begin to take off my costume and become who I really am. Thank you for making me and for knowing me as I am. Teach me to love myself as you love me. Thank you for life, and thank you for loving me just as I am today. For all these things I pray. Amen.

November: A Time for Reflection and the Giving of Thanks

John 3:16, Ephesians 1:7, 2 Corinthians 5:17

November: What a wonderful month! Fall is a time for us to stop and see God's beauty in the world around us. It's a time to be with family, to have fellowship with one another, a time to laugh, and a time to make memories. It's a time to stop and reflect on our blessings throughout the year and to give thanks to God for all He has given us. Even if we have a loved one who isn't with us, we can still thank God for those memories we do have and thank Him for the time we spent with the one who meant so much to us. The fall is a time of reflection and a time for thanks.

As I reflect on the month of November, lots of things come to mind: football games, lots of food, sharing, birthdays, and even death. As I take time to give thanks, I find that my blessings are so bountiful. I sometimes feel as if God has blessed me more than I deserve. I have health, a wonderful family, beautiful grandchildren, a home, a car, and the list goes on and on. I also thank the Lord every day for my church family. My church, as well as another church, has played an important part in my life and for that I am blessed.

In the dictionary thanks is defined as "an expression of gratitude." Gratitude is explained as "an appreciation for favors received." The dictionary explains favor as "a kind act, a small gift or token." I could keep going, but to get to the point, being thankful means appreciating what people have done for you or what they have given to you. Most of the time in church, we are asked to stop and give "thanks" for our blessings. One of our first responses always seems to be for our families, our homes, etc. Somewhere down the list, we finally get around to mentioning God and what He has done, but for many people He is not on the top of the list.

Since November is a time of reflecting, I think we should stop and reflect on what God has done for us, but not only then—year round. If you are reading this then you are alive. We each should be thankful for the time we have here on Earth. We are never promised tomorrow, so we should live life each day to its fullest and be thankful at the end of the day. If you are reading this then you are blessed with eyesight. Even though it may not be what it was a year ago, we should be thankful for the sight we do have.

Another favor we have received from God that we didn't deserve or ask for was the gift of God's Son, Jesus. God gave each of us a token of His love by sending His only son to this Earth to die for us. When He died on the cross we became new creatures; our sins were not only washed away, but God forgot about them. This Thanksgiving look around your table; look at your family and friends. If God asked you to sacrifice one of your family members just as He did, could you do it? Which one of the family members would you be willing to give up? As you ponder this, remember one thing: the one you choose will not be a sacrifice for just your family, but for all of humankind. That includes prostitutes, murderers, the guy at work who you don't get along with, the people in Africa that you don't know, the thugs sitting in jail, and your next-door neighbor. It will be a sacrifice for everyone. The sad part of it is even though you offer your relative for a sacrifice, not everyone will accept the gift. Now how does that make you feel? Even though God offered His son as a sacrifice to wipe away every sin committed, there are people who still don't know Him or won't accept Him. There is not one of us who would be willing to make that sacrifice, but God did. He did it for you and me and everyone else.

NOVEMBER: A TIME FOR REFLECTION AND THE GIVING OF THANKS ᕽ

This Thanksgiving as we are once again asked to stop and give "thanks," let us thank God for His ultimate gift of life and His forgiveness of our sins. Let each of us take a few minutes, whether it is November or otherwise, to reflect and give thanks to God for His goodness to us.

"For God loved the world so much that he gave his one and only Son, so that everyone who believes in him will not perish but have eternal life. God sent his Son into the world not to judge the world, but to save the world through him."

John 3:16-17

Prayer: Dear Lord, as I sit around the table looking at my family and friends, I know in my heart that I can't sacrifice them. I am not willing to let them die for people I don't know or for those who I don't think deserve life. Yet, God, that is what you did. You sent your only son to die for me. You did this not only for me, but also for those who I don't know, those who I judge as not deserving of your love. You died to wash away the sins I have committed and those I will commit. You died so I might have life eternally. All you ask for in return is my love, and for me to love unconditionally those you have put in my midst. You ask me to forgive and be forgiven. You give so much to me, yet you ask for so little. I thank you for your Son, my family and friends. I thank you for the blessings you pour out on me each day. I honor you with my life and my love. I lift your name in praise and thanksgiving for all you do for me, in Jesus' name. Amen.

Christmas of a Different Kind

Luke 1:26-2:20

The year 2005 found my husband and me celebrating Christmas in Texas for the first time, and it was different. I remember that on November 28 it was 58 degrees. I wasn't used to that. I have always known the Christmas season to be cold, snowy, and chilling. I like snow. I don't like ice. I like snow when I am decorating for Christmas or Christmas shopping, and I definitely want a "white Christmas." These things are not connected with Texas. A couple of weeks ago, I asked someone from Texas if it ever got cold. I wanted it to be cold so that I could get in the "mood" for Christmas. She just laughed. My husband and I laughed about how hard it was going to be to decorate the outside of our home for Christmas in T-shirts instead of winter coats. Would Christmas really seem like Christmas?

That's when, once again, God's nudging began. He shared His thoughts with me. And once again, it was nothing I didn't already know. I had been taught all my life how Christmas is not about the snow, the gifts or the worldly celebration. It was about the celebration of God's gift to us, His only Son. Did I really practice what I believed? So many times I have written articles on how to celebrate the "true meaning of Christmas," but did I really put it into practice? Unfortunately, I realized I hadn't. You see, Christmas has always been about the snow, shopping, and gift-giving. I depended on my external circumstances to get me in the "mood" for Christmas. Now, being in Texas, I realized that was all wrong. You see, there is no snow or freezing temperatures to get me in the mood. I soon realized that was the world's idea of a perfect Christmas, not God's, and it shouldn't be mine either. You turn on the radio and what do you hear? Songs like "Let it Snow" or "I'm Dreaming of a White Christmas," but nowhere does it say in the Bible that there was snow when Christ was born. I had allowed my circumstances and the world outside to dictate when I would get in the mood for Christmas. Now how would I get in the mood? Simply by remembering what Christmas is all about and putting it into practice. I would have to make myself practice the art of Christmas, not only believing what I have known all along, but also practicing it. I would have to learn to look inside my heart and remember to celebrate not just Christmas, but really celebrate Christ's birth. I would have to look on the inside and draw on God's love and the true meaning of Christmas.

I use to buy lots of gifts for my kids at Christmas. I wasn't happy with them getting only one or two—it was usually several gifts apiece. One year for Christmas, I was upset because we had to cut back. One of my girls reminded me it wasn't about the gifts; it was about us being together. The next year, I went back and did the same thing again. In 2005, because we were going to have to travel, I couldn't buy as many gifts for each of them (also, with all the little precious jewels God gave to us that year, it would get expensive). They would have Christmas, but not as abundantly as before. Along with finding the true meaning of Christmas, I have also realized it means giving of ourselves. It is truly as the girls said, "It's not about the gifts, but us being together." Since we are separated by many miles, I realize now that the best gift I can give them is my love and my presence at Christmas. It is *really* about sharing one's love with each other. It's about sharing memories, tears, and laughter. It's about sharing dreams, hopes, and fears with one another. It's about loving and caring. I bet none of you can name all the gifts you got for Christmas last year and who gave them to you, but I bet you remember the

CHRISTMAS OF A DIFFERENT KIND

time your family got together and the friends that came to visit. Give yourself to others. Share God's love and the celebration of God's birth with others.

So, yes that Christmas was different, but it was exciting. As I decorated for Christmas in my short-sleeved shirt, I knew that it wasn't about the snow or about the freezing temperatures. Christmas is truly a celebration of Jesus' birth. As I shopped for gifts, I gladly cut back, knowing it wasn't about gift giving, but sharing God's love with all my family and friends. It would be about wrapping up my fears, hopes, and dreams into a package and giving them to Jesus. It would be about receiving God's gift and taking time to unwrap His present and enjoying the life He has given me.

Do you practice what you believe? Do you practice the art of Christmas? Do you give of yourself instead of gifts? Do you depend on snow to get you in the mood? I hope each of you find a way to make Christmas meaningful this year. May you share your dreams, hopes, and fears with your families. Take time to unwrap the most precious gift God gave us, His Son. Take the time to understand fully what it meant for God to give us His Son. Make this year a time to truly share God's greatest blessing with each other. Celebrate Christ's birthday and not just Christmas!

> *"They entered the house and saw the child with his mother, Mary, and they bowed down and worshiped him. Then they opened their treasure chests and gave him gifts of gold, frankincense, and myrrh."*
>
> *Matthew 2:11*

Prayer: Dear God, in this materialistic world, I forget what Christmas is all about. I go to the stores and I am caught up in the buying and the rushing around. I let the world dictate my life and think I have to do it all. As I visit family and friends I rush about. I hustle from one home to another, never taking the time to stop and reflect on what Christmas is all about. Teach me to pause and remember it is about the birth of your Son. It is about your gift to me. It is about your Son being born so I may have life eternally. Help me not to get caught up in the gift giving but instead in the giving of myself to others. Thank you, Lord that you teach me in everyday circumstances how to live for you. Slow me down this Christmas and allow me to experience the true meaning. Happy Birthday, Jesus! Amen.

Taking Off the Comfortable and Wearing the Uncomfortable

James 1:22, Psalm 37:23 ━━━━━━━━━━━━━━━━━━━━

Growing in Christ is not an easy thing to do. Just about the time you get comfortable with how things are going in your life, God begins to make things uncomfortable again. It takes time to adjust to the new things God has planned for you. Every few months or years I find this out. I compare it to buying a new pair of shoes. I know I am a little nutty, but read on and see if you don't agree.

A few weeks ago I noticed my "old faithful–stand–by" tennis shoes were beginning to hurt my feet. They had grown uncomfortable and not too pretty to look at. I needed new ones. I don't like to buy new shoes because it takes a while to break them in and feel comfortable—it takes them awhile to become "old faithful." It seems that just about the time they get to be comfortable, they become ugly and worn out.

That's how it is with our faith. When we first become Christians, it is not an easy thing for us. It is uncomfortable. God starts working on us and getting rid of those awful, ugly bad habits we have acquired. Those we are comfortable with. It can take some of us some time to adjust to the changes. Sometimes it even hurts. We are comfortable with doing those things and we seem to hate breaking the habit. Or maybe God asks us to change our relationships because they aren't healthy for us. We hate breaking relationships even though we know that sometimes it's in our best interest. It hurts!

Just about the time we get involved in church and start participating and becoming comfortable with who we are and what we are doing, our faith begins to feel uncomfortable. It can take us a while to figure out what's going on. Then we suddenly realize we have outgrown our comfortableness. We begin to struggle with where we are and what we are doing. We know we must change our faith and we know we must seek out new areas for our faith to grow. Sometimes we go on a spiritual retreat, or we go to the altar and seek a closer relationship, or we get involved in a deep Bible study that challenges us to change. Then what happens when we begin to change? We get uncomfortable again. We begin to feel the pinching, the tightness, and even the snug feeling. As we grow closer in Christ, we find it's not as bad as our first change, but it is still uncomfortable.

Then it happens all over again, and again, and again. That's the way it should be. We should never be comfortable for too long with our faith. We need to seek change, to grow, and to become stronger every year in our faith. Just about the time you think you are comfortable, it is time to ask God to help you become uncomfortable again. We always should be asking Him to help us find areas in our lives where we can improve. It might be in our witnessing to others, or in our giving, or our mission work, or maybe just in how we treat others. He might ask you to begin changing your worshiping habits, like attending more often, or becoming more intense. None of us knows what God has planned.

I know for myself (and through the years) my faith has only grown when I begin to feel uncomfortable with how I am presently living. I know when it is time to take off the comfortable and begin living uncomfortably for a while. It is during those uncomfortable times I can look ahead and know the comfort is coming soon—I must just be patient and wait. That is my prayer for you today. How about being uncomfortable for a while with me and watch as our faith grows?

TAKING OFF THE COMFORTABLE AND WEARING THE UNCOMFORTABLE ➤

"Put on your new nature, created to be like God—truly righteous and holy."

Ephesians 4:24

"Instead, we will speak the truth in love, growing in every way more and more like Christ, who is the head of his body, the church."

Ephesians 4:15

Prayer: Dear Lord, it is not always easy to take off the old and put on the new. Change can be hard for me to deal with. I like to feel comfortable. Growing can cause growing pains. Growing sometimes means I must leave old things behind and move into new areas that can be strange and different. It seems that just as I begin to get comfortable, you call me to stretch and grow. Help me to be ready to take off the old and put on the new. Give me courage to move forward, trusting you as I go. Thank you, Lord for the opportunity to grow more like you each day. Amen.

What Is Normal?

Proverbs 1:23

Life had been pretty hectic for several months. Kids were getting married, kids were moving, and a daughter was home from college for the summer. Our lives were turned upside down and we had no normal routine. As life began to settle down for us, I was eager for things to return to normal. What is normal? Life was changing and "normal" would no longer *be* normal. We would have to discover a new normal for us. You know what I'm talking about. Your kids have left home; you don't have the normal wash load. You normally washed clothes two or three times a week just so your daughter or son could wear his favorite outfit, but now it seems you are doing the laundry once a week. Normally you never got the bathroom to yourself and now you do. You routinely never got to answer the phone. Now there is no one to answer the phone if you don't.

Different ones began to ask if I was anxious about the future. Would "empty nest syndrome" bother me? No, I was excited! That may sound strange, but I was. There were a number of reasons for my excitement. There were things I had put on the back burner because I was busy raising children. Now I would have time to do those things.

One of the things I had put on the back burner was discerning

God's will for my life. In fact, I had just started reading a book on how to discern God's will for my life. It explained how to distinguish God's voice from my own and that of the world's. My goal in life is to live for Christ and to do His will.

I didn't know at the time what that was and I didn't know where that would lead me. I had complete trust in my God knowing He was in control. He would never lead me down a path where He wouldn't go with me. To me that's an awesome thought, knowing God has prepared and is preparing the way for me.

In the Bible Discipleship Study that we had just finished, we talked about giving up "control" of our lives. We all agreed that too many people want to hang on to that concept of controlling their lives. They just can't stand the thought of someone or something else controlling them. We as Christians must give up *complete* control of our lives, not just a part of it, but *completely*. In order to do that, we must first surrender our lives to Christ. Ask for forgiveness, then seek salvation in Christ, and then trust Him on a daily basis for our every need. In Philippians 3:3 it says, *"For we who worship by the Spirit of God are the ones who are truly circumcised. We rely on what Christ Jesus has done for us. We put no confidence in human effort."* Maybe part of trusting God is coming to the place where we realize there is nothing we can do for ourselves anymore. We have to rely on God for everything.

We also need to read our Bibles on a daily basis. How can we know what God wants for our lives if we never read His Word? My husband's favorite saying is, "If all else fails read the instructions." My saying is, "Read the instructions before all else fails." If we read the instructions before we fail and we follow those instructions, we can't fail. God won't let us fail unless it wasn't His will to begin with. Read the Bible, know God's Word, and keep it in your heart. I had treasured the last two years I was in Bible Discipleship Study, mainly because I had to study His Word, and now I am better equipped to know His will.

Prayer is just another step in knowing God's will for our lives. We cannot do God's will if we don't ask Him what it is He wants for

WHAT IS NORMAL?

us. Prayer, for me, is a two way street. One way is talking to God, the other way is listening. We have to go both ways to get where He wants us to go. We have to be willing to be silent and listen for God. He may use circumstances and people to show us His will. We must be open to those around us and be aware of the circumstances that open for us. It may be God opening doors.

Remember, another important part of discerning God's will for our lives is being willing to do His will, no matter what it is. What is the use of asking God to show us His will for our lives, if we don't plan to carry it out? If we are going to seek His will, we must trust God enough to say yes even before we know what it is. Just like Moses and Jonah we can argue, but in the end we must be willing and have a willing heart to do His will. God will not allow us to do anything we can't handle together.

Are you ready to prayerfully consider asking God what His will is for your life? Are you willing to seek and carry it out? I hope so. Together we can seek His will and serve a risen Savior.

> "Teach me to do your will, for you are my God. May your gracious Spirit lead me forward on a firm footing. For the glory of your name, O Lord, preserve my life. Because of your faithfulness, bring me out of this distress."
>
> Psalm 143:10-11

> "Don't act thoughtlessly, but understand what the Lord wants you to do."
>
> Ephesians 5:17

Prayer: Dear Lord, I want to give you control, but it is not easy. I like being in charge, yet at times I make a mess of things. Give me the courage to allow you to be in charge and give up control of my life. I often wonder what your will is for my life, but I am too afraid to ask. I am afraid you will ask me to do things I can't do. I know, Lord, that if you want me to do something for you, you will equip me. Help me to seek your will for my life. Help me to move out, and not only seek your will, but be ready to do your will. You have prepared the way for me and you will never let me walk alone. Grant me the courage and the peace to move out and do what you are calling me to do. Thank you for the knowledge that I can trust you to do what you say. Thank you for your promises! Show me now, Lord, your will for my life. Amen.

Me Walk on Water, Are You Kidding?

Philippians 4:13

It amazes me how God uses circumstances to talk with us, to convey His message to us. About a month before we left for a vacation, I had the opportunity to share lunch with my sister. We went that afternoon to a Christian bookstore, which is dangerous for my pocketbook. I envisioned picking up another book from my favorite author. Well, another book by an author I didn't recognize caught my eye. John Ortberg is the author and the book is *If You Want to Walk on Water, You've Got to Get Out of the Boat*. I found the title interesting, read a small part of it, and realized I had been talking on this same subject on Wednesday nights—stepping out of your comfort zone. I couldn't resist. I bought the book. I was spellbound by the book for several weeks before leaving for vacation. Everything I needed to hear was in that book. If you are looking for a challenge and want to step out of your comfort zone, I recommend it. This is a life-changing book. The week before we left, the sermon was on the topic "stepping out of your comfort zone." How odd, I thought, but I didn't continue to think much about it.

We went to the Atlantic Ocean, and the book is based on Peter getting out of the boat and walking on the water. Later, I was reading this book at the beach when I looked up and all I saw was water.

It began to become real as I watched the tide come in and go out. There were days the water was really rough, and I could really begin to understand Peter's fear of the water, as He took His eyes off of Christ and looked at the waves crashing around him. I thought about how odd it was that these three events were related: me buying the book, the sermon, and now being at the ocean. All right, it was probably just a coincidence, I thought. Then, we decided to go to church in Florida. I went inside, opened my bulletin, and to my amazement the minister has been doing a sermon series dealing with Peter getting out of the boat and walking on the water. He hadn't finished the series and that is what the scripture and sermon were for that day. Now I am beginning to feel uneasy and start wondering what God is planning for me next.

After vacation, I returned home, read some more of my book, and the second week I was in church after vacation, the pastor at the time decided to use that as his message and scripture. Wow! I could only wonder what was going on. I started praying for some answers to the many questions I had, but the one answer I got in return was, "Wait." So, I assumed that in His time I was to know when I was to get out of the boat and start walking on water.

In the meantime, one of the phrases John uses in his book is the one I hang on to—one for us all to think about and cling to. Paraphrased, it goes something like this: It is better to be *out of the boat* and *with Christ* then to be *in the boat without Christ*. The question is being raised for us all to think about. Is it better to be safe and in the boat without Christ, or is it better for us to respond to Christ when He tells us to "come" and be out there with Him? If we stay in the boat we are safe, comfortable, and most likely out of danger, but Christ isn't in the boat with us. We are sitting there in our boat all nice, comfortable, and safe. We look at others walking on the water thinking, "Man, are they stupid or what? They can't walk on the water, don't they know that? They are doing some really crazy things." What they don't realize is if they look around, Christ isn't in the boat with them. He's out there asking each of us to take courage and come to Him. It is only when Peter takes his eyes off Christ and looks around that Peter starts getting into trouble. If you know anything about the life of Christ, Jesus never seems to take the comfortable, safe route for anything. He was always treading water. Just like the story about feeding the thousands; the comfortable and safe thing to do was send the people away to fend for themselves. Instead, Christ takes five loaves of bread and two fish and feeds the people. There are several examples of Christ doing the unsafe, uncomfortable thing. That is what I believe He is calling each of us to do today. He is calling us to get out of the boat and join Him. We are confined to the boat and can't do a whole lot while we are sitting in there; however, if we get out of the boat, there is a whole big area where we can go and walk on water. The other thing we are assured of is this: if we keep our eyes on Christ, we can't fail. It is only when we take our eyes off Christ and look at our circumstances that we begin to fail. For some of us we realize it is better to be out of the boat *with* Christ than to be safe and comfortable *without* Christ.

Maybe each of us needs to look at our own comfort zone and walking-on-water level. Are you willing to take that first step after God calls you and walk on the water, knowing He will be there with you? Or is it your desire to stay safe and comfortable and let God keep calling you?

The answer for all of us is a very simple one: let each of us answer God's calling. Let's step out of the boat, walk on the water, keep our eyes on Christ and experience what God can do with us, the church, and those around us as we tread water. Let us together answer God's calling and step out of the boat and do some water-walking.

> "Then Jesus said to his disciples, 'If any of you wants to be my follower, you must turn from your selfish ways, take up your cross, and follow me.'"
>
> Matthew 16:24

L.T. FROG

"Then Peter called to him, 'Lord, if it's really you, tell me to come to you, walking on the water.'

'Yes, come,' Jesus said. So Peter went over the side of the boat and walked on the water toward Jesus."

Matthew 14:28-29

Prayer: Dear Lord, it is not easy to do what you call me to do. It is not easy to take that first step out of the boat. I know you are outside the boat waiting for me, and that is where I truly want to be. The world, my family, and friends are yelling at me to get back in the boat. "It's not safe out there!" they say. But I know if I keep my eyes on you, I will be fine. It is only when I take my eyes off you that I begin to sink. I thank you for being here, calling me to take that first step. Put the desire in my heart to listen to you. Teach me to be a Peter and trust in you only and always. Thank you for insight into your words. I love you, Lord, and I praise you for what you are doing in my life. I ask all these things in your name. Amen.

Haiti

Matthew 25:34-46

Five of my friends and I had the opportunity to visit Haiti on a mission trip in October 2001. Wow! What an experience the five of us had. After September 11, I was not looking forward to going. I was frightened, yet I couldn't put my finger on why. I even prayed the trip would be canceled, but it wasn't, so on we traveled. It seemed like it took us forever to get there. What was waiting for us was an experience I will never forget. There are so many experiences to tell. I met so many people who I will never forget. We heard amazing stories from missionaries who told how God placed each one of them in Haiti. Their stories tell me that God is still working in people's lives today. He is still seeking willing hearts, willing hands and feet, and willing bodies to do His work.

I have always been in church. I have heard lots of missionaries speak, and some of them even spoke about Haiti. One thing I was always told as a child is how you can be in a different country and not speak the language, but still attend a church service and experience God's presence and His Spirit as people from different cultures worship together. I could hardly believe that was possible. We went to Wednesday night church service in Haiti. They had already started worshiping as we arrived. We didn't know the language so we couldn't sing along. But guess what? I knew Christ was in that service and His Spirit was among those people. I could feel His presence as I sat for the first time and listened to others singing and praying. You could look into the men and women's faces and see the same Christ I serve on a daily basis. These were my brothers and sisters in Christ! Someday I will be with them in Heaven. Then we can sing and share together in the same language, and we will share the love we have for Christ with each other.

As I watched my daughter intermingle with the Haitian children, I couldn't help but see the love on their faces and on hers. The love of Christ is something so simple, yet so precious.

At one point, we visited a housewife. Christian Services International, or CSI (the group we visited that was working in Haiti), had built her and her husband a new home. The look of pride from this woman as she showed us around her home is something I will never forget. It wasn't fancy, but it was clean and it was nice and it was hers. God had blessed her, and she knew it and gave Him all the praise and glory.

We met a doctor who had given up a practice in Florida to go to Haiti. Why? Because God said "go," and he did just that. He was not sponsored by any group; just by friends and people who care. He lives on what people send Him. He is trusting God to provide, and God is providing. The love he shows as he cares for the sick, injured, and hurt people of Haiti is evident in his eyes and audible in his voice as he shares. We were a part of a miracle while we were in Haiti. Can you imagine being a part of a miracle? We were, and that in itself was worth the trip. A man came to the house and told us he had lost some valuable items, some of which were identification items. We prayed that God would intervene and help find the things the man lost. In the next few days, he arrived back praising God. God had answered our prayers. He found everything he lost.

What have I come away with? So much I can't put into words. I have experienced and seen God's love and His work in action. I know that no matter how I feel today or tomorrow, God is actively working in people's lives. I know also that I am truly blessed to be living in a country of opportunity. In Haiti, there is little opportunity for many. I watched as people sat and did nothing, because there was nothing for them to do. They had very little. Most of them slept on the ground. No one had running water or bathrooms. Some of the children had no clothes, and very few had many possessions. Were they an unhappy people? No. Most of them were content with what they had and with their lifestyles. There was laughter in the streets and in the homes we visited.

In America we strive for more and more. In Haiti there is no striving. They are content with what they have.

My plan is to return to Haiti someday to work on a site. I want to work beside the Haitian people and share our love of Christ with each other and share in worship again.

For now, it is my desire to have a closer walk with Him. I am asking to be used by Him, to be His feet, His hands, and His body to do the things He wants me to do. I wish everyone would consider going on a mission trip somewhere, even if it is in their own city. In many of our own towns and cities, there is mission work to be done. It may be in a senior citizens center, or a youth center, or in the inner city; but there is something for you to do. Ask God to lead you. He is not shy about telling you where to go. Go where God is needed because the message needs to be heard. Go where you dare not go on your own, but where God leads. It says in the Bible in Matthew 28:19-20:

> *"Therefore, go and make disciples of all the nations, baptizing them in the name of the Father and the Son and the Holy Spirit. Teach these new disciples to obey all the commands I have given you. And be sure of this: I am with you always, even to the end of the age."*

Prayerfully consider asking God to use you. Then, don't be afraid and don't look back. Just become a "frog" and *fully rely on God*, and He will truly bless you.

"Then these righteous ones will reply, 'Lord, when did we ever see you hungry and feed you? Or thirsty and give you something to drink? Or a stranger and show you hospitality? Or naked and give you clothing? When did we ever see you sick or in prison and visit you?'"

"And the King will say, 'I tell you the truth, when you did it to one of the least of these my brothers and sisters, you were doing it to me!'"

Matthew 25:37-40

Prayer: Dear Lord, it is not easy to leave my comfortable home and bed, or to go on a mission trip. I don't always want to see how other people live—it can hurt too much. I think I am too busy or I am not qualified, but all it takes is a desire to do your work and a love for your people. Give me a desire to reach out to those who need a healing touch, a kind word, or to hear about God's love for them. Thank you for those men and women who have made mission work a lifestyle. I ask your blessings on their lives, as well as protection. Grant them wisdom, knowledge, and strength as they reach out to your people. I ask all these things in thy name. Amen.

Sharing Your Faith, What a Breeze

Matthew 28:16

I have found on more than one occasion someone telling me they don't know how to share their faith. I admit I have been perplexed with this idea, too, but recently I found out how easy it can be. We all can share our faith with one simple task.

I shared one of my frogs that I had received with a special "friend" (who is more like an adopted sister). This friend was having surgery and she wanted a frog to remind her to *fully rely on God*. She set it by her bedside, and she wrote me an email and told me she had several nurses ask her about it. She even said one of the nurses wrote it down so she could remember it. Well, that was an open door for my friend to share her faith. How easy was that?

Needless to say that got my brain to thinking. This is what I came up with (or should I say this is what God shared with me). Each of us needs to find our "frog" item. What I mean by that is maybe your item won't be a frog, but you can pick something that relates to your faith. Something small you can put in your pocket to carry around with you, something that is unusual. Then when you are around someone and you want to share your faith, take it out of your pocket and see what happens.

I will share some of the items I thought about. I know as creative as all of you are, you can come up with one on your own.

How about putting a small rock in your pocket? In Psalm 71:3 it says, "*Be my rock of safety where I can always hide. . . for you are my rock and my fortress.*" When I think of a rock, I think about how God is as solid as a rock. He will never fail me. He will always be there for me. And like rocks, we are all different, but in God's eyes we are the same and He loves us the same. Our friendships with others sometimes crumble and are not always solid, but our relationship with God will always be solid as a rock.

How about carrying about a piece of magnet in your pocket? When people see you with a magnet they are going to think you are one of those "health nuts" who believe in magnets (and maybe you are). Instead, you can use this opportunity to tell them that God's love is like a magnet: Once you have experienced it, you want to cling to it and never be away from it. There are many ways to share your faith using a magnet.

Or how about carrying a tiny bear around with you? When I think of bears I think of bear hugs. Having God in your life on a daily basis is like getting a bear hug every day.

Whatever you use should be a reflection of your faith. That way it will be easy to share your faith with someone instead of always trying to remember what your item stands for. I also suggest it not be a cross or a religious item. People see those items and sometimes shrink away. You want something that will draw people's attention to it. It needs to be unusual, something to make people ask about it. I stress this: it must be about your faith—something you can relate to.

My family and friends have picked up on this, too. I have received several frog items, including necklaces, statues for the inside and outside of my home, and bookmarks. People often comment, "Oh, you like frogs?" That gives me the chance to tell them why I like frogs. You should see the look on people's faces as I pull out a small frog from my pocket when I need change. As I dig in my hand to give them the correct change, the frog is there. I jump at the chance to tell them why I am carrying a frog in my pocket.

In I Peter 3:15-16 it says:

"*Instead, you must worship Christ as Lord of your life. And if*

SHARING YOUR FAITH, WHAT A BREEZE

someone asks about your Christian hope, always be ready to explain it. But do this in a gentle and respectful way. Keep your conscience clear. Then if people speak against you, they will be ashamed when they see what a good life you live because you belong to Christ."

We are to be ready and able to share God's love and salvation with everyone at anytime.

If all of us found an item and started sharing our faith, it wouldn't take long for our churches in America to grow and for our nation to once again be a Christian nation. With the events happening in our country, people are going to begin looking for something in which to put their faith. What better way for each of us to start sharing our faith with the world? If you think about it, this is an easy and very simple way for all of us to share God's message. Take time to find your item, and then start sharing your faith. Share your faith with your family and friends and see how long it takes for your collection to grow into something special for God.

"And then he told them, 'Go into all the world and preach the Good News to everyone. Anyone who believes and is baptized will be saved. But anyone who refuses to believe will be condemned.'"

Mark 16:15-16

Prayer: Dear God, I thank you for sending your Son to die on the cross for my sins. It is not enough to say thanks. I must share salvation with others. Thank you for the hope and the trust I have found in you. I must share with others that same hope and trust. Every day, give me the opportunity to share with others what you have done for me. Thank you for frogs that can be used to help me share my faith. Work through me; give me words as I share my faith. Amen.

What an Awesome God!

Genesis 1

God is an awesome God! My husband and I went on vacation and visited eight states and some of the most beautiful country I have ever seen. The eight states were Iowa, Nebraska, South Dakota, Wyoming, Colorado, Kansas, Missouri, and Illinois. There was something unique in each state. We visited the Badlands, Black Hills, Mount Rushmore, Devils Tower, the Rocky Mountains, and Dodge City.

As we were leaving that week, I heard briefly on the news something about the Big Bang Theory and how they were going to explain how the world was started.

After visiting these sights, I know how the world was created. Only God could create something this beautiful and wonderful. If you have never been to the Badlands, it is hard to explain. The Badlands is comprised of formations and no two formations are alike. The color is something to behold and to grasp. That was probably my favorite place. It reminded me of human beings. No two are alike; we are all different, and in our own way we are all beautiful people. You can look at a formation and then move and look at the same formation and it looks different. That is the same way we are. We never stay the same. We are always changing.

Looking at the formations, you don't know which ones have defects and which ones were created that way. That is the way it should be with us—we should never see the defects in people. We should only see God's creation in others.

There are pine trees as you travel through Mount Rushmore, and the aroma of those pine trees is wonderful. It was wonderful to have the window down to smell such a pleasant, sweet smell. I'll never forget it. It reminds me of the lady in the Bible who poured the perfume on Jesus' feet. I bet the aroma was just as sweet. Mount Rushmore was my husband's favorite. The mountain alone was worth seeing, but then to see the faces of those presidents carved into the side of the mountain was breathtaking. We were there close to Independence Day, and there were celebrations going on. To see the Native Americans dance and to hear them sing was inspiring—to know that long ago this land belonged to them and that this was their home.

As we traveled on, we stopped at Devils Tower and heard the legend of the children playing there. We saw the prayer cloths hanging in the trees and were asked to leave them alone and to respect those that had hung them there. How could anyone or anything create something so unique and beautiful? It just had to be God's handiwork.

We came back and stopped at Dodge City. Even though Dodge City was now a reenactment, I stopped and thought about all those who had traveled out West. All those men, women, and children who had traveled in covered wagons just so people like us could experience the West. All of those who suffered diseases and many other obstacles as they traveled; just so God's creation could be made known to us. Wow! History comes alive!

There is beauty in the world all around us. We don't have to travel from state to state to see it. The problem is, we are so used to seeing our little corner of the world on a daily basis that we can't see the beauty around us. So what happens? Visitors come to our corner of the world and see our beauty and tell us how beautiful it is and we go, "Are you nuts? This is just Indiana (or whatever state

WHAT AN AWESOME GOD!

you are from)." After you have traveled for fourteen or fifteen days and then go home, you can see the beauty in your corner of the world. It is always good to visit other places and to see new things, but it is also good to be home. There used to be a song that says something like "take time to stop and smell the roses." I am asking each of you, no matter where you live, to stop and take time to see the beauty around you. Look at God's creation. If you live in town, take a drive out of town and drive down some old country roads. If you are from the country, take a Sunday or an afternoon and drive to town; see the sights, and visit with old friends.

There is a song we often sing (especially at church camp) called "This Is My Father's World." I love singing that song because it does remind me that this *is* His world, and if we listen, we can hear Him rustle in the grass and hear Him pass. There is another song some of us may have sung called "For the Beauty of the Earth." The refrain says, "Lord of all, to thee we raise this our hymn of grateful praise." We should praise God for the beauty of Earth and even for our little corners of the world.

My prayer and hope for each of you is that this very day you will see the Earth's beauty and tonight as you go to bed, offer a prayer of praise to God for His creation.

> *"Then God looked over all he had made, and he saw that it was very good. And evening passed and morning came, marking the sixth day."*
>
> *Genesis 1:31*

Prayer: Oh, Lord, your world is beautiful. I am sometimes too busy to stop and look at your creation. I rush about and miss all that you have given me. I take for granted those things around me. It is only when I go on vacation or when I am forced to stop, that I find the beauty around me. Open my eyes to your world and help me find the beauty in the creation you have provided for me. I thank you for the beauty of a clear, blue sky; and for

L.T. FROG

those dark gray clouds that bring me rain. I honor you as I look at the majestic mountains, knowing it was you who created those for my world. I thank you for the oceans and the seas, and the fields where farmers plant their crops. This is my Father's world; help me to see the beauty in it. Amen.

McVeigh Dies — Judgment Day

II Corinthians 5:10

Timothy McVeigh died a little after 7 a.m. on June 11, 2001. He is dead. The execution was the top news story that morning as I got ready to go to work. Some people were happy, some were sad, some were in disbelief, and some were just quiet.

I am not here to give you my views on capital punishment. I am not here to say we were right or wrong. I am here to express my thoughts on his death.

When they announced his death, I thought, Oh my, he is now meeting the God who created him. The God who gave him a brain to think with, hands to use, a mouth to speak, ears to hear and eyes to see.

I felt sorry for Timothy. He was meeting the God who would determine where he would spend eternity. He would have to answer questions, explain his actions, and then face his eternal future. Maybe sometime he repented, accepted the Lord, and became a Christian. Maybe we will meet him again in Heaven. Maybe we will not. That is not my judgment call (thank you, God, that it is your call). It remains: He will have to answer to someone bigger than you and me.

We will also. Although I have known all my life I will meet my

God and I will be judged for my actions, my words, and my thoughts, it didn't hit home until that day. It became a reality for me. I began to think about how I have treated people, what I have said about people, and what I have thought. What will happen when I meet my maker? What will my eternal future be? Timothy destroyed many lives, but how many lives have I destroyed because of something I said or did?

The Bible says, *"For we must all stand before Christ to be judged. We will each receive whatever we deserve for the good or evil we have done in this earthly body"* (II Corinthians 5:10). Not some of us, but all of us will be judged. When we get to Heaven and the book with our names is opened and God begins to judge us, will we be ready? Will we have to explain our actions? Will we be ready to answer the questions that will be set before us? Will we be ready to accept our eternal future? If not, now is the time to get ready. If you noticed, the Scripture says "good or bad." God will take note of all the good things we have done. Have I done more good than bad? If I could make a list of all the things I have done all my life, which list would be longer?

Timothy knew when he would die. He had time to prepare. We don't know when our time is coming. It may be today, tomorrow, next week, or next year. Whenever, we must prepare today. We must be ready for our own judgment days.

It is too late for Timothy McVeigh, but it is not too late for us. Don't put off something that needs to be done today. Take time to evaluate your life and decide if you're ready to meet your God if He called you home today.

My prayer that day and now is for those in Oklahoma, Timothy's family, and those who witnessed his death. It is also for each of you. My hope for you is that you know where you will be spending your eternal future. My prayer is that if you are uncertain about where you will spend eternity, you will seek God while God is seeking you. Let's plan on spending eternity in Heaven together.

"So you, too, must keep watch! For you don't know what day your Lord is coming."

Matthew 24:42

"You also must be ready all the time, for the Son of Man will come when least expected."

Matthew 24:44

Prayer: Dear God, I will have to answer to you for the things I did and didn't do here on Earth. Make me aware of my thoughts, actions, and words. Remind me to be alert each day, preparing my life for my judgment day. Help me to not only offer forgiveness, but to also forget what others have done to me. Let me reach out in love to those around me. Thank you for sending your Son so my sins will be forgiven and forgotten. I love you, God, and want to serve you daily in all I do. Amen.

Finding Calmness in a Hectic World!

Mark 6:46

One year, we traveled out west for our vacation. We took our daughter, son-in-law, and granddaughter with us. Some of the places we visited that year we had visited two years earlier. We went on to Yellowstone and Old Faithful, as well as some other places we hadn't seen before. It was my desire to show them the Badlands. We once again camped at the same place we had before. The owners treated us like we were old friends. It was great seeing and talking to them again.

While visiting the Badlands, I made a comment to my son-in-law that I didn't know what it was about the Badlands that made them my favorite place to visit. There are pull-offs throughout the park where you can park your vehicle and get out and view the scenery. As we got out of the truck, I had this desire to talk quietly and to just sit and take it all in. My son-in-law later told me he had an answer to the comment I had made. He told me the Badlands had a calming effect. He felt the same way. It's as though you want to just be calm and let nature wrap itself around you. It is an awesome feeling. Even when things are hectic around you, you feel at peace there. If you get a chance to experience the Badlands, take it.

◂ L.T. FROG

One morning after returning home from vacation, I was getting ready for work. I had my breakfast fixed and decided to sit on my porch swing and enjoy a few minutes of peace and quiet. As I sat there I listened to the birds singing, the water running from our fountain, and all the other morning noises. I was suddenly taken in by my own surroundings. I was wrapped up in nature in my own yard. It was a wonderful, peaceful, calming effect. I realized that as nice as it was, I didn't need the Badlands to achieve that same calm. At the Badlands, I also felt I could see God, see His creation, and experience His world in a whole new way. That morning as I looked about, I saw God's creation all around me. I could feel the heat from the sun. I could hear the birds chirping praises to God, and I could smell the wonderful smell of summer. I could sit on my porch and still feel God's presence. I could experience His world in a fresh new way. Why hadn't I had this experience before?

Well, to be perfectly honest I had this experience a few years earlier, but had lost it. Why? Because I had been so consumed with being, doing, and going that I hadn't taken the time to relax and let God fill me with His peace. I had been so busy that year that I hadn't taken time to stop and smell the proverbial roses. I had been so busy doing for my family, doing for my church those things I felt needed to be done, and going here and there to do things I thought were important. I was so busy being a wife, a mother, a secretary, a grandmother, and being a Christian that I hadn't taken the time to just sit with God and be quiet in His presence.

We all need to take some time to just sit and feel God's presence and to experience God's creation. You don't have to go to the Badlands. You don't have to run out and buy a swing. All you need to do is find a favorite place where you can be by yourself outside in God's world. Don't take a book or the newspaper to read, don't take music to listen to (God's provided all the music you need), and you don't need anyone to go with you. Let it be just you and God. Allow God to fill you with His presence. Allow Him to calm you, and then be open to those things around you that God has created for us to enjoy. The birds' chirping will sound clearer, the air will be fresher, and His creation will look brighter. Soon, you will be filled with an awareness of God's love for you and a peace that surpasses all understanding. You will once again be renewed and stronger than you have been for a while.

Even Jesus had to get away for awhile. In Mark 6:46 it says, *"After telling everyone good-bye, he went up into the hills by himself to pray."* In Matthew 14:13 it says, *"As soon as Jesus heard the news, he left in a boat to a remote area to be alone. . ."* Again, John 6:15 tells us, *"When Jesus saw that they were ready to force him to be their king, he slipped away into the hills by himself."* These are just some examples of Jesus going off by Himself to pray and meditate. If Jesus needed this time, doesn't it only make sense that we need this time, too? We are not any better than Jesus.

This month, find some time to get off by yourself. Find your "special" place, meditate, pray, and allow nature to wrap itself around you and allow the calmness to take over. Listen as God and nature talks to you and fills you with peace. Then come back rest-assured that you will be ready to take on the world and all that the devil throws at you. God bless, and enjoy your time "in the Lord."

"The apostles returned to Jesus from their ministry tour and told him all they had done and taught. Then Jesus said, "Let's go off by ourselves to a quiet place and rest awhile." He said this because there were so many people coming and going that Jesus and his apostles didn't even have time to eat. So they left by boat for a quiet place, where they could be alone."

Mark 6:30-32

Prayer: Dear God, I don't often take the time to be alone with you. When I pray, I am so busy asking for things that I seldom listen to you. Your Son needed time alone to rest, to regain strength, and to find comfort in you. I need those same things today. Help me find that quiet place where I can go and be alone with you. And when I am in my quiet place, help me to open my ears so that I may hear you, and open my eyes so that I may see you. I thank you for those times that I can come and just be alone with you to worship you, to praise you, and to love you. Amen.

What Does God Expect From Us?

Micah 6:8

I recently have come across a text in the Bible that I really like. I am sure I have read it before, but it really hit home this time. It is found in Micah 6:8. It reads, *"No, O people, the Lord has told you what is good, and this is what he requires of you: to do what is right, to love mercy, and to walk humbly with your God."*

How can something so simple be so hard to do? Very clearly God tells us what He wants from us. The first thing He expects from us, according to this Scripture, is to do what is right to other people. How hard can that be? We are to treat others just as we would like to be treated. How many of us want to be yelled at? How many of us want to be cheated on? Stop and think about how you treat others. Do you treat them like you would want to be treated? If you got everything in return that you gave someone else, would you be okay with that? Too many times we forget that how we say things or how we do things affects other people. Not just those close to us, but everyone we come in contact with. If we have had a bad day, we often take it out on the clerk waiting on us or the first person in our path. How would you feel if someone passed their bad day on to you? By mistreating the clerk (or whoever the poor victim is), that puts her in a bad mood. So what does she do? She passes her bad day on to the next customer. On and on it goes. Wouldn't it be wonderful if all of us who were having a good day passed our good day on to others? It's just like the contagious smile. If one person smiles and says hello to the stranger she passes on the street, that very well might get passed on to the next one and so on. As you come into contact with people, stop before you act or speak. Say to yourself, "Is this the way I would want to be treated?" We often tell our kids, "Treat others the way you want them to treat you," but many times as adults we ignore that piece of advice. The "do as I say, not as I do" mindset comes into play. I think if we all treated others like we would like to be treated, this world would be much nicer and there would be less hatred and mistrust.

The next thing God wants from us is to love being kind to others. It is easy being kind to our family and friends. If one of our family or one of our friends needs a ride to the doctor's office or hospital, we are right there for them. Think about the stranger who needs help. As a church secretary, many times I would ask for help from our congregation with transportation to and from the hospital for others. How many takers did I get? No one offered to help. Why? Because no one knew the person asking for help, or if they knew them, they weren't willing to take the time from their busy day to help someone who wasn't a friend or family member. We don't want to go the extra mile anymore for others unless we think we might get something out of it. Kindness is not running rampant these days. If kindness were running rampant then there would be no more road rage, would there? Can you imagine what would happen if we tried to out-do each other with acts of kindness? Can you imagine how much better this world would be if we all did our share of kindness? All God wants us to do is love being kind to others. There is so much competition these days. What would happen if we all really did start competing against each other with our acts of kindness? You would be surprised at the blessing you may receive from being kind to others.

The next simple thing God tell us is to live humbly. We are all so busy trying to get a bigger home, or a better car. We want more and more for our families. When we strive to get ahead and have nicer things, we sometimes neglect God. How? By working more and more hours each week, we have no time for church or to do the things God wants us to do. Many people spend hours and hours on their lawns getting them to look just "picture perfect." How about taking some of those hours and doing some acts of kindness? Or reading the Bible? How about devoting those hours we spend on the lawn to a Bible study group? If we aren't working on our lawns then we are spending money getting someone else to work on our lawns. What if we took that extra money and used it to feed a family who is in need? Or what if we helped young families with their bills? Or maybe a young person who is trying to find money to go to college?

We are to live humbly which means to live modestly. The next time you make a purchase or you think you need to replace something with a bigger, newer item: ask yourself whether it's really necessary or whether it's something to brag about to your neighbors and friends. One of the things I have started trying to do when I buy something is ask myself how God could help me use this item to help others. For instance, I have bought a couple of cars in my day. So, I tell God if He ever has need of my car it is His. There has been more than one occasion where someone needed to borrow my car or needed a lift, and I was able to provide it. When it came to clothes, I was stumped. My daughter came up with the perfect solution. When I buy something new I have to get rid of an older item in my closet. I take those gently used items and give them to people who are homeless.

What about those hours you waste doing something that is not necessary, like playing on a computer, watching TV, window shopping, or spending excessive amounts of time on the golf course, basketball court, or the baseball field? Couldn't we find better ways to serve God? I believe in having a good time and enjoying one's self, but when we say we haven't got any time for the things God wants us to do, but spend hours and hours doing the things we want and like to do, it becomes a problem.

Finally, God wants us to obey Him. This simply means if God is asking you to do something, if He is asking you to change your ways, then we should listen to Him and do what He wants. Obey in the Webster's dictionary is defined as "be guided by." That is what God wants from us. He wants us to be guided by His desires for our lives. We can only do that if we know Him, listen to Him, read His Word, and worship Him. We must learn to put our own agendas aside and allow God's agenda for our lives to take over.

How well are you doing? Are there areas you could improve on? God doesn't expect much from us, but there are things He wants from us. These are just a few. What can God expect from you? This month, let us encourage one another to apply this Scripture to our lives.

> *"Finally, all of you should be of one mind. Sympathize with each other. Love each other as brothers and sisters. Be tenderhearted, and keep a humble attitude. Don't repay evil for evil. Don't retaliate with insults when people insult you. Instead, pay them back with a blessing. That is what God has called you to do, and he will bless you for it."*

I Peter 3:8-9

Prayer: Dear Lord, it is much easier to strike back when I have been hurt. It is human nature to insult someone after I have been insulted. I think I will feel better if I repay evil for evil. Often times, I feel worse and I am sorry for my actions and words. Teach me to turn the other cheek and to repay evil with kindness. You forgave those who put you on the cross for my sins. Put the desire in my heart to do well toward others, to love them unconditionally, and to obey you. I ask all these things in thy name. Amen.

A Personal Relationship—What's Up With That?

John 10:27, I John 2:3-6

I have come to the belief that many people have a "relationship" with God. I think we all want to claim we have a relationship with God. Even those who don't attend church on Sunday will tell you that, yes, they believe in God and some may even say they pray. They think if they believe in God and go to church a couple times a year that is having a relationship with Him. The problem is, we have relationships with all kinds of people every day. We can have a relationship with the mailman. A friendship can develop by just saying hi or asking about his family and friends. We can have a relationship with our doctor. That is a relationship we only share once in awhile unless we have to visit him or her on a regular basis. We have relationships with our dentist, hairdresser, car repairman; and these days we can have a relationship with our computer. Some people spend as much time on the computer as they do with their spouse or mate.

So what's wrong with these relationships? Not a thing, as long as they don't develop into something that will hurt us or harm someone else. The problem lies in that God does not want us to have just any relationship with Him.

Well, if God does not want us to have just *any* relationship with

Him, exactly what *does* He want? A *personal* relationship is what He longs for from each of us. According to Webster, personal means "carried on between individuals directly." Now, my explanation is "carrying on a relationship with another person directly on a day-to-day basis or even a minute-by-minute basis."

Stop and think about your relationship with your mate or your children. It is almost imperative that you have a personal relationship with them. You deal with them, think about them, and live with them seven days a week, twenty-four hours a day. Even with your married children, you still have that personal relationship with them. You are constantly interacting with them, talking to them, asking their opinions about things and sharing with them. It is personal. My children and grandchildren live several states away, yet I maintain a personal relationship with them.

Stop and think if you had the kind of relationship with your children or mate that you do with your mailman, doctor, or dentist. You would only interact once in a while with them. You wouldn't spend time with them. You wouldn't share a meal with them. You really wouldn't know them.

Getting personal means learning all about them. When you get personal with those you love, you find out their likes and dislikes, you find out what makes them tick. You find out (or at least should) what makes them angry or mad and you try to avoid doing those things. You can read them like a book. You know whom they hang out with, where they go and what they do. You listen to them, talk to them, share with them, and you laugh and cry with them. For some spouses, they can finish a sentence the other has started. That is what God wants. He wants to laugh with us, cry with us, and talk with us; and He wants us to listen to Him. He wants to "hang out" with us on a daily basis.

I believe too many people in our church pews today have a relationship with God, but it is not truly personal. It is not the kind He wants. We come in on Sunday mornings for an hour or so to listen to the minister preach and sing a few songs and go home feeling good about ourselves. We don't enter the door of the church until

A PERSONAL RELATIONSHIP—WHAT'S UP WITH THAT?

the following Sunday unless someone has stuck us on a committee. We don't open our Bibles, pray, or attend any services during the week. When someone asks us if we have a relationship with God we say yes. Ask yourself, is it the same kind of relationship we have with our loved ones here on Earth? If not, then we should seek out that kind of relationship. We should seek to have a better relationship with God than the mailman. We are missing something if we don't have a personal relationship with Him. He can't cry with us if we don't share our sadness with Him. He can't laugh with us if we don't share our joy with Him. He certainly can't "hang out" with us if we leave Him at the church doors each Sunday.

Too many times we seek God only when our lives are a mess. When our lives are crumbling, that is when we want to know He is there for us. When our lives are going just fine, we think we don't need to check in. When life is going fine for me is when I need Him the most and can often times feel His presence in my life.

Check on your relationships. Make a list and see how many relationships you have. Then check your "personal" relationship list. Is God on that list? If He is, where on that list is He? Is He at the top or the bottom? Let's all develop a personal relationship with God and become once again a Christian nation.

> *"'Not everyone who calls out to me, 'Lord! Lord!' will enter the Kingdom of Heaven. Only those who actually do the will of my Father in heaven will enter. On judgment day many will say to me, 'Lord! Lord! We prophesied in your name and cast out demons in your name and performed many miracles in your name.' But I will reply, 'I never knew you. Get away from me, you who break God's laws.'"*
>
> Matthew 7:21-23

Prayer: Dear God, I know your desire for me is to have a personal relationship with you. In the busyness of this world I often do not take time to have relationships. Even with my own family I struggle finding time for them. My work keeps me away from church, the evening news and my favorite shows keep me from spending time in your Word. I may think I know you, but I am not sure. Give me the desire to have a personal relationship with you, so on judgment day you will say to me, "Well done good and faithful servant, welcome home." I ask all these things in thy name. Amen.

Are You Prepared for the Celebration?

Matthew 25:1-13

One Sunday our pastor preached on the story of the ten virgins, found in Matthew 25. He preached about how they had to be ready for when the bridegroom returned. No one knew when he would return. If they were ready when he returned, they would be invited into the celebration. I began to think about how it related to my own life. My daughter was expecting our first grandchild during that time. We had been given a general idea of when the baby was due, but Rebekah Rose would make her appearance when God said it was time. Only God knows when we are to be born and when we are to die. Rebekah could come in the middle of the night, in the middle of the day, or early in the morning. She could come any day of the week from Monday to Sunday. She could come during worship service, while I was at work, shopping, in meetings, or anywhere. Only God knew when she was to be born. In the meantime while we waited, what were we, as family and friends, to do? Well, nothing really. We went on about our work. There was no sense in stopping what we did to wait. We could have waited a day, a week, or several weeks. We kept busy doing what we were called to do. Her parents, on the other hand, were busy preparing for her birth; finishing up the room, getting diapers ready, and making the dry run.

None of us know what time or when Christ will come to take us home. We are to be ready whenever we receive that call. That's exactly what the pastor was talking about.

So far, I have not found (but then again I am not looking, either) any books on preparing me to be the best grandmother I can be. I know some things I can do to be the best. I had some wonderful grandparents who taught me a lot. I now have some wonderful friends who mentor me on being the best grandparent I can be. My own mother was a wonderful grandmother to my children; and now my friend, Lila, has taken her place and has mentored me on being the best I can be, not only as a grandmother, but as a person.

In the Christian life, we are to be about God's work while we are waiting on Him to take us home. We are to be about studying His Word and gaining wisdom. We are to be about encouraging others. We are to give financially to God's service. We are to be in prayer at all times. We are to be prepared in every way.

In the parable of the ten virgins, five of them were prepared and took oil with them; and the other five took oil but did not have enough to last until the bridegroom came. If we are to be prepared, we have to be like the five who were prepared. We can't be like the five virgins and have just enough religion or faith to hold us over for a short time, hoping He'll call us home soon. Too many of us decide that we have read the Bible enough, we have been in enough Bible studies to last a lifetime, we have worked in the church long enough, and it is now time for someone else to take over. When it comes to daily devotions, we think if we've been in church the week before it should last until the next week. We don't need a daily filling up. Or the best one I have heard is this line, "With all the time my mother and father have spent in church, I should be okay," or, "They have given enough money to the church to last through their lifetime and mine. I don't need to do anymore. They have done enough." Just because our parents were saved and they gave to the church, it doesn't mean we will be saved. Our parents' faith can't save us.

ARE YOU PREPARED FOR THE CELEBRATION?

Look at what happened to the five who weren't prepared. The oil ran out. They had to go fill their lamps up. While they were gone, the bridegroom came. When they realized what had happened, they asked to be part of the celebration, but the bridegroom said no.

It may be hard work carrying the load of extra oil. I know. Sometimes you don't feel like praying, or reading the Bible. There are times you think it would be better to stay home than go worship in church on Sunday mornings. You don't feel like being with others, and besides, that the bed is much more comfortable than a pew. Sometimes you just get tired and want to quit. Do you want to miss out on the celebration? Do you really want to miss out on what the bridegroom has in store for you?

Be prepared at all times—that is the message God is telling us in this story. Don't get to a certain age or time in your life where you think you are ready; likewise, don't get too tired and think you're ready. We are not the ones to judge whether we are ready. I have a friend who is dying from cancer. He was a minister. He knows he will be spending eternity with God. He is ready to go home, yet God has not called him home. So, John waits. Now, knowing John I am sure he is still praying, reading his Bible, and sharing God's message with those who come to see him. He has not stopped doing what God has called him to do. He is still preparing himself and others to meet God. John's favorite line is, "Praise the Lord." Many who have gone to see him during his last days told me that he still praises God.

In Matthew 24:42 it says, "So you, too, must keep watch! For you don't know what day your Lord is coming."

It was a lot easier for me to prepare myself for being a grandmother than for being a faithful servant. While I enjoy being a grandmother, the rewards will be greater if I keep preparing myself for Christ's return, whenever that will be.

Won't you join me in preparing for Christ's return? Let us be ready together and enjoy the celebration Christ has waiting for us.

L.T. FROG

"But he called back, 'Believe me, I don't know you!'

'So you, too, must keep watch! For you do not know the day or hour of my return.'"

Matthew 25:12-13

Prayer: Dear Lord, I do not want to miss the celebration you have for me when you come back. Yet, I am so busy with life, children, jobs, sports, and other things that I am not ready. I think I have plenty of time. No one knows when you will return. You want me to be ready today, not tomorrow. Help me to realize that I have today and I am not promised tomorrow. Thank you for the celebration you are preparing for me. Help me as each day I prepare for your coming. I ask all these things in thy name. Amen.

A Deeper Relationship with Christ

Romans 8:28

A deeper relationship with Christ—does that idea scare you? It scares me. Let me explain. I never could understand why people were afraid to have a deeper relationship with Christ. To me, that would be the ultimate, to grow more every day and to have this deep relationship with Christ. Wow! I thought that would be wonderful. Now I have to wonder.

I am growing right now. As my mom would say, I am going through a growth spurt. I should be excited right? Well, I am not sure.

I am excited because it is a wonderful feeling knowing I don't have to rely on myself. Instead, I can *fully rely on God*. Knowing that God is in control and I no longer need to fear or worry about the future is wonderful, but—wait a minute—there is another side to the story.

Now for the scary part of having a deeper relationship with Christ: I believe this part keeps many Christians from having one. When you begin to develop a deeper relationship with God, you lose control and have no idea where God is leading you. Sounds pretty scary don't it, having no control over your life? As you grow deeper in your faith and you rely more and more on God, you have no idea where you might end up. I realized this one morning as I was reflecting on my walk with Christ. To tell you the truth, it scares me when I think of where I have come from and then not knowing where I am going. I would have been most comfortable staying where I was a year ago, but I had this idea that I wanted to grow closer to God and to have a deeper relationship with Him. As I pursued that goal, I did not think about the consequences; the consequence of allowing God to so move in my life that I had no clue as to where I would be headed.

I have now realized having a deeper relationship with Christ means allowing Him to move you where He wants you to be. It also means doing what He desires and obeying Him to the fullest extent! How scary is that?

As we grow closer, He asks us to step out of our comfort zones and do His will, be His witness, His hands, and His feet. He even wants us to speak for Him. He demands we put Him first, leaving everything else behind Him. For me, that meant family, sorority, and anything else that was a stumbling block in my relationship with Him.

That is where many of us are. We want that deeper relationship with Christ but we are not willing to sacrifice our control. I think, also, we really don't want those "stumbling blocks" moved. We enjoy our families, our jobs and our social organizations. If we move into a deeper relationship, we have different priorities and different goals. We look at people in a different manner; we find we are no longer in control. So, instead, we stay where we are. We just dream and wish for a deeper relationship. We may even envy others because they have something we don't have.

I had just finished my first Lay Speaker Ministry class and I was scared all over again. I had no idea where God was leading me. What keeps me going? Why do I do it if it scares me? Because at the same time it is exciting—it is an adventure. In the end, I know where I will be. I will be where God wants me to be and I know who will be in control. It is also because I know God is in control and leading me all the way. He will never lead me where He will not go first to prepare the way for me.

Have you been given the opportunity to grow closer to God, to

A DEEPER RELATIONSHIP WITH CHRIST

have that deeper relationship with Him? Do you desire to have a closer relationship with Him? It is all in the giving up of the control of your life. My prayer for you is that you step out in faith, step out of your comfort zone, and allow God to take control of your life. The thing is, it can be a wonderful scary feeling. It's like that feeling you get on a roller coaster, or when you get married, or when you become a parent for the first time. You feel wonderful but at the same time, a little scared. You get excited because you are about to take that plunge, yet, at the same time deep down you have a scary feeling building up in you. Because I have given God control of my life, I have been places I would never have gone, I have done things I never would have done, and I said things to people I would never have said. I don't regret a minute of it. It is awesome to see where God has led me, and I am just as excited about where He is leading me. Yes, it is a wonderful, exciting time.

Consider joining me for what promises to be an exciting life in Christ.

"'For I know the plans I have for you,' says the Lord. 'They are plans for good and not for disaster, to give you a future and a hope. In those days when you pray, I will listen. If you look for me wholeheartedly, you will find me.'"

Jeremiah 29:11-13

Prayer: Dear God, it is not easy to step aside and let you have complete control of my life. It is a scary feeling for me. I give you some pieces of my life, but I hold some back. That is not what you want from me. You want complete surrender. As I begin to surrender my life to you, I must trust you also. I know that whatever you call me to do, you will be there with me, guiding me along the way. I give you praise! Thank you for guiding my step in the past. I surrender my life to you. I ask you to take control of my life, giving you all the honor and praise for who you are and who I will be in you. Amen.

Dropping Things and Letting Go!

Mark 8:34-35

One year in February, my husband came home from work and announced the plant where he worked would be closed for a week and we were headed to Florida. You just don't come home and tell a well-organized woman she is going on an unscheduled trip and she only has a couple of days to get ready.

After arriving in Florida, I realized how organized I really was. I am not bragging, just stating a fact. I also realized I am *too* organized for my own good. I can look at my calendar and tell you what I am supposed to be doing a week from now. This leaves no room for flexibility. No room for husbands to come home with plans to go on an unscheduled trip.

When my husband told me we were leaving for Florida and I had three or four days to get ready, this threw me into frenzy. This was impossible for me. I had meetings to go to (since I was a church secretary), bulletins to do. I had to find someone to fill in for me, and let the pastor know I was going to be gone for a week or so. Since we would be taking the camper, we needed to get it ready. We needed to put our clothes in the camper and buy groceries and put them away. At the time, I was taking care of my dad, which meant I had to find someone to fill in for me. Someone would have to come and check on him once in a while. How could I accomplish all of this in just a few days? It seemed impossible. I found all kinds of excuses for why we couldn't just pick up and go. However, my husband insisted. He was going to leave and I could either go with him or I could stay home, attend my meetings, work, and live a neat orderly life while he was enjoying the sun and the warmth of Florida in February. To add to all of this, it was going to be our first vacation without the kids. Although they were young adults and could take care of themselves, I wasn't sure about leaving without them. It wasn't that I didn't trust them—I just had never left them. They had always gone with us. How could I leave them?

As I was on my way to Florida, I wondered what I would have done if Jesus had been the one to ask me to drop things and go on a trip. What would I have done if He had asked me to drop my schedule to help someone in need? Would I have argued with Him? Would I have given Him as many excuses about not going as I did Greg, my husband?

The disciples were asked to drop their nets and follow Jesus. They did. They did not argue with Him. They did not get their life figured out before they left. They did not go home to say goodbye to their family and friends. They just left. Could I do that? Could you?

In Luke 9:61-62 it says, "*Another said, 'Yes, Lord, I will follow you, but first let me say good-bye to my family.' But Jesus told him, 'Anyone who puts a hand to the plow and then looks back is not fit for the Kingdom of God.'*"

Our lives, including mine, need to be flexible enough to go when God says go, to do when God says do. My goal for this year is to be more flexible and allow God to be a part of my life in such a way that if He needs to send me, I can be sent. I do not want to worry about schedules, meetings, and being so organized that I have to say no to Him. I don't worry about canceling dates now, or changing plans. That is all in the past. Now I am ready to say, "Yes, Lord, send me."

How organized is your life? If God asks you to go somewhere without a minute's notice, could you go? It may be as simple as

DROPPING THINGS AND LETTING GO!

dropping things and going to the hospital to visit someone, or to the nursing home, or taking someone to a doctor's appointment; or, yes, even to a mission field. Could you go? Would you be willing to be a disciple for Christ? How do you plan on responding when God calls?

> *"Another said, 'Yes, Lord, I will follow you, but first let me say good-bye to my family.' But Jesus told him, 'Anyone who puts a hand to the plow and then looks back is not fit for the Kingdom of God.'"*
>
> *Luke 9:61-62*

Prayer: Dear Lord, it isn't easy to throw out my calendar and follow you. It isn't easy just to go when you say go or do when you say do. I know when you call me I must be ready to do those things you have need for me to do. I am your hands, your feet, your ears, and even your mouth. I must be ready to serve you at a minute's notice. Help me to be flexible enough to say, "Yes, Lord, I will go and serve thee." Thank you for those times you have been there for me, now let me be there for others. Amen.

Good Stuff or Junk

1 Peter 2:1, Galatians 5:22

A few years ago on my day off, I was beginning to make room for my father-in-law. He was going to move in with us. One of the things I decided to do that day was discard some things I really didn't need. I do this every fall, anyhow. I am sure Goodwill really loves me. Somehow, I always manage to take over at least a carload of stuff. As I began to clean out some of my things that year, I noticed the whole household got in the act and they followed my lead. So, I not only had my things, but also my daughters' things to deliver.

This particular time, I was going through my clothes. If I hadn't worn a particular item during the summer, it was history. Or, if it had stains on it and looked pretty bad, it was gone also. A lot of us take time during the year to go through our closets, cabinets, and other storage areas to get rid of stuff. Sometimes we even wonder why we bought some of the stuff we did. We keep what we think is valuable and get rid of what we call junk. These days our junk is other people's treasure.

How many times do we do this in our own lives? How often do we take the time to go through our lives and discard the junk and keep the good stuff?

Do we even realize what is good and bad in our lives? One way to find out what we need to hang onto or get rid of is by consulting God. We first must go to Him and ask Him what areas in our lives are areas that need to be cleaned out. Let Him show us what we need to get rid of. There maybe things we have or things we do that just need a bit of straightening out. For example, suppose we set a time each day to watch our favorite soap opera (or for me, its game shows or Court TV); that's not bad. Maybe, though, God will ask us to take that same time slot and instead of watching TV, read the Bible, do devotions, or spend time in prayer. Which would benefit us more, the soap opera or daily devotions?

Maybe we spend each morning calling our friends to find out what we missed the night before. That is not a bad thing as long as we don't gossip. What if, instead of finding out what we missed last night, we use that time to call a friend who is lonely, or a shut-in who never gets out, or we call someone who might need a prayer that morning? You can certainly pray with someone over the phone.

These are some areas that are good, but just need straightening out. God may point out some areas where we just need to clean out some things. For instance, if we are really good at judging others God may decide it is time we got rid of that area of our life. We are not to judge others' actions, thoughts, or deeds. We are to leave the judging to God. James 4:12 says, *"God alone, who gave the law, is the Judge. He alone has the power to save or to destroy. So what right do you have to judge your neighbor?"*

Or how about those areas where we hold a grudge against someone? We are not to hold grudges toward anyone. God may ask us to seek out those we hold a grudge against, resolve the problem and then get rid of it. James 5:9 says, *"Don't grumble about each other, brothers and sisters, or you will be judged. For look—the Judge is standing at the door!"*

I know that in my own life, I need to re-evaluate the things I have accumulated. I know there are habits I form that I need to discard. There are some things I need to keep and make better use of. I also have found out this is a yearly project. Just like those clothes that we get rid of, I manage to add some to take their places. You think you have gotten rid of all the clothes you have outgrown or stained and then you find another one has taken its place. That is the same way with bad habits or bad areas of our lives. You think you have them all cleaned up and slowly they creep back in or something else comes in and takes their places. If you don't take time to get rid of those areas or those bad habits, they will finally consume your life until you have no room for the "good stuff."

In I Peter 2:1 it says, "*So get rid of all evil behavior. Be done with all deceit, hypocrisy, jealousy, and all unkind speech.*" Those are the things we need to rid ourselves of. In Galatians 5:22-23 it says, "*But the Holy Spirit produces this kind of fruit in our lives: love, joy, peace, patience, kindness, goodness, faithfulness, gentleness, and self-control. . . .Against such things there is no law.*" We are to replace those things we got rid of with kindness, goodness, and all those things mentioned in Galatians. Why should we hang onto jealousy, petty thoughts, or grudges? They are like stains on our clothes. God says get rid of them, so we should. Out they go, with all the other junk in our lives.

Have you cleaned the bad stuff out of your life lately? Let us each reevaluate our lives and keep only those things that are of value to our Christian walk with God.

"So get rid of all evil behavior. Be done with all deceit, hypocrisy, jealousy, and all unkind speech."

I Peter 2:1

"But the Holy Spirit produces this kind of fruit in our lives: love, joy, peace, patience, kindness, goodness, faithfulness, gentleness, and self-control. . . ."

Galatians 5:22

◄ L.T. FROG

Prayer: Dear Heavenly Father, it is time I looked inside myself to see what I need to rid myself of. Make me aware of those areas in my life that need a good cleaning. Help me to replace the junk in my life with the fruit of the Spirit. Old habits are hard to break, but with you as my guide, I can do all things through you. Thank you for showing me those areas that need changing. It is my desire to serve you and I can't serve you, Lord, with junk in my life. Thank you for all you are doing in my life. Amen.

How Do You Communicate?

Ephesians 6:18

If asked, most people would say open communication is one of the most important attributes of a friendship. You can't have a friendship with someone if you don't talk to them and they don't talk back.

Can you imagine having a loving relationship with your husband, wife, mother, father, or child and never talk to them? What kind of friendship would you have if you only talked to that person when you were troubled or in need of something? Or how would the friendship go if you did all the talking and never listened?

Open communication is important in all relationships and friendships, but how often do we neglect the opportunity of having open communication with God? How often do we go to God in prayer? When we do go, is it just when we need something or when we're troubled or need healing for friends or family? Do we do all the talking and pleading?

To have a relationship we cherish and thrive on, we must communicate with that person on a daily basis. It is the same way with God. We can't go to God only when we need Him, when our family needs Him, or we are in trouble. It has to be an everyday thing with God.

In a relationship we can't do all the talking, either. The person we'd want to have a relationship with would get pretty tired and disgusted with us. Having two-way communication is as important as having open communication. We must listen to what God is telling us, as well as talking to Him.

The Bible says in Luke 18:1, "*One day Jesus told his disciples a story to show that they should always pray and never give up.*" In I Thessalonians 5:17 it says, "*Never stop praying.*" In Colossians 4:2 it says, "*Devote yourselves to prayer with an alert mind and a thankful heart.*" In all of these texts, it says we are to pray all the time. We are not just to pray when we feel the need, but continually. If you are having trouble with prayer, remember it is no more difficult than talking to a friend. As you pray, think of God as your best friend, someone you feel comfortable with and can talk to. I have even heard of people pulling up a chair next to them and talking as if God is sitting in that chair. Don't feel you have to use "churchy" words. That's not what is important to God. In Matthew 6:5-7 it says:

> "*When you pray, don't be like the hypocrites who love to pray publicly on street corners and in the synagogues where everyone can see them. I tell you the truth, that is all the reward they will ever get. But when you pray, go away by yourself, shut the door behind you, and pray to your Father in private. Then your Father, who sees everything, will reward you. When you pray, don't babble on and on as people of other religions do. They think their prayers are answered merely by repeating their words again and again.*"

That says it pretty clearly doesn't it? We are not to be like those who go on and on. How many times have you been somewhere and heard someone pray and they go on and on and on? It's like the Energizer Bunny. God doesn't want that. He knows what's in our hearts. He just wants us to be simple, pure in our asking, but most of all, honest. What is important is just sitting down and chatting back and forth with Him. Telling Him what you are thankful for, your concerns and taking the time to praise Him. Talking to God is just like talking to a friend. The more you pray to God the easier it becomes. Before long you will find yourself in constant prayer throughout the day, sometimes doing one-liners. You will find yourself saying a prayer as you drive down the road. Sometimes a person pops into my head and I offer up a prayer for him or her. I will drive by an accident, see an ambulance, or hear the fire trucks and offer up a prayer for those involved. It is just simple communication with God, just as you would with a friend.

As you would listen to a friend, it is just as important to listen to God. You will probably not hear a voice like you hear your friend's voice, but He will communicate with you. You may decide to read the Bible one day, when God impresses you to read a certain text. When you do, often times it will be the answer you were waiting on. A lot of times when I am in my car, I will turn off the radio and just listen for God to speak. Although I don't hear a voice sometimes a solution to a problem will come to me and I'll know it was from God, even though I didn't hear Him. I know in my heart it was He who revealed it to me. Sometimes God will speak through friends. I have been sitting in church on Sunday morning and God has spoken to me through the sermon or the music or someone's testimony. Sometimes God uses books to get through to us. Whatever means He uses, it is important to listen to Him.

If you stop and think about some of the long friendships that have lasted through the years, it is because we have stayed in touch, shared good times and bad times, and have been there for each other through it all. That is exactly what God wants from our relationship. God wants someone who takes the time to care and share their good times with Him and their bad times with Him. He wants those who will devote themselves to Him.

Every night before I go to bed I pray. Now, sometimes I fall asleep and when I wake up I remember where I left off and start again. I pray for safe traveling for my husband and sons-in-law as they go to work. Before I jump out of bed, I say a prayer for the day. You'd be surprised how much easier the day goes when it starts with prayer.

Prayer is the key to a long, loving relationship with God. How is your prayer life? How is your relationship with God? Try praying today; it will improve your relationship with our Heavenly Father.

"I urge you, first of all, to pray for all people. Ask God to help them; intercede on their behalf, and give thanks for them. . . In every place of worship, I want men to pray with holy hands lifted up to God, free from anger and controversy."

I Timothy 2:1, 8

Prayer: Dear Lord, it is good to come to you in prayer. You taught your disciples how to pray and I follow their example praying, *"Our Father which art in heaven, Hallowed be thy name. Thy kingdom come, thy will be done in earth, as it is in heaven. Give us this day our daily bread. And forgive us our debts, as we forgive our debtors. And lead us not into temptation, but deliver us from evil: For thine is the kingdom, and the power, and the glory, for ever. Amen."* (Matthew 6:9-13, KJV).

Make Disciples

Matthew 28:19-20

The church I attended for several years decided to develop a mission statement at one point. Each Sunday in church service, we would repeat the mission statement. I believe they thought if we said it often enough and believed in it, the church would fulfill their mission. The mission statement they had chosen went like this: "The mission of this church is to make disciples for Jesus Christ."

I began to wonder how many of us even knew what it meant to be a disciple, let alone believed in it? What is a disciple? In the Webster dictionary it is described as "one who accepts and assists in spreading the doctrines of another."

So, in layman's terms it means one who decides to accept the Christian faith and goes on to help spread that Christian faith. Now, according to this mission statement my church adopted, they were to help make disciples for Jesus Christ. My question for that church and any other church is, "Are we doing that?" Are we truly leading others to walk with Christ and then encouraging them to witness to others? How can we encourage others to witness when we don't always witness ourselves?

My daughter came to me once and said, "Mom, I don't feel I have a witness. I have nothing to share. I have been in church all my life. I've never had a traumatic experience. What can I share?" Later we went on a Lay Witness Mission Weekend together. This is a weekend where several people from different communities go to a church and we share our witness with the people of that congregation. We make disciples for Christ. My daughter shared her Christian walk with some of the people during the weekend. I don't know exactly what she shared. God does and so do the people she witnessed to. I don't need to know. It is not important that I know. What is important is that: 1.) she witnessed, and 2.) she made others realize they can witness, also. She had one lady come up and tell her, "I didn't realize it, but I can witness about my faith too."

We do not have to have a dramatic or traumatic story to tell. We do not have to have a tear-jerking experience to share with others. All we need to do is share our story. Our faith story is what Christ has done for us. We can share with others what Christ is doing in our lives. I had been in this church for a while now. There were some people who had not shared their Christian walk with me. I had never heard some of the people from that congregation say what God had done for them or what He meant to them. I know I would have been encouraged, and I would have gained strength and help from it. Maybe you have gone through something in life I haven't gone through yet, but in the future I may have to. How will I know how to get through it if you don't share with me how Christ got you through it?

It is just as important to share our faith, as it is to read the Bible, pray, go to church and tithe. If we are ashamed of God and we are afraid of telling others about Christ, Christ will be ashamed of us on our day of judgment. II Timothy says we are not to be ashamed to testify (or witness) about our Lord.

Once we share our faith, we must begin to encourage others to share theirs. One of the things we did during the Lay Witness weekend was to pair off with one another. Once we paired off, we shared our Christian walks with each other. It is so easy to just sit and share with one another. We don't even realize we are doing it until we have done it. Then we realize just how easy it is. Everyone is into exercise now. What if we changed the way we exercise? What if, instead of physically

MAKE DISCIPLES

exercising, we exercised in a different way? For example, each week we seek out someone who we have not shared very much with. Take them to lunch, buy them a Coke, or take them on a walk around the neighborhood. While you are with them, encourage them to share their Christian walk with you. Ask them questions, get them to open up. You may even want to start out sharing your own walk with them. Get to know them and find out what Christ is doing in their life. You might just find out they are going through some rough times and something you say might help them. Or maybe they don't have a relationship with Christ. They can't witness to you if they don't have one. This would be a great time to share with them what Christ can do for them.

On more than one occasion, someone's faith story has encouraged me, strengthened me, or made me more aware of how God is working in my own life.

I encourage each of you to take the time to share your witness with just one other person this week or this month. Then encourage one other person to share their witness with you. As we encourage one another, we will begin to make disciples for Jesus Christ; and our mission statement will be an active part of our life and not just a statement.

"I tell you the truth, everyone who acknowledges me publicly here on earth, the Son of Man will also acknowledge in the presence of God's angels. But anyone who denies me here on earth will be denied before God's angels."

Luke 12:8-9

Prayer: Dear God, thank you for all you are doing in my life. I am grateful for those times you have helped me through difficult situations. Send those people into my life who need to hear my faith stories. Give me the words to share with others. Help me to be opened to those around me that need to hear about you. You shared your Son with me, now let me share your Son with others through word and deed. Amen.

Spiritual Warfare

II Corinthians 10:3-6

When I was younger, I heard ministers talk about "spiritual warfare." I was never certain what it was. Unfortunately, I can now say, I not only know what it is, but I have been attacked. Listening to some of my friends talk, they have, too.

Spiritual warfare is an experience of being attacked by the devil using any means he can. After returning from my Walk to Emmaus, I went through all kinds of minor anguish. I have noticed the closer I get to God, the more I experience spiritual warfare. I was used by God to get a Wednesday evening prayer and praise service started and that, too, was a target of spiritual warfare.

The devil will use whatever means it takes to fight us, to keep us from getting closer to God, or from even having a relationship with God. While I was trying to organize this midweek service, I was having some medical tests done. After finding out that the results of the tests were not good, knowing I was going to have to see another doctor, and having the possibility of surgery, the devil decided to use that to attack me. He tried to persuade me that I was depressed. He brought in several factors relating to this incident. After a few minutes, I was getting depressed. He even had me close to tears. I was feeling useless, worthless, and insignificant. A few minutes later, realizing what the devil had done, I decided to use spiritual warfare myself. I called on God, sang praise songs, and did whatever it took to defeat the devil. I won! With God's help, I won the battle that the devil had fought so hard.

I now realize the closer I get to God, the more the devil will try to fight me. Have you experienced spiritual warfare? I also have noticed that even in church, the devil will try to start a spiritual war. We had gone through a dry period when the Holy Spirit was missing from our worship service. People had left church, and it was getting to become a desperate situation. We were in a financial slump and things were going downhill really fast. I am sure the devil was having a heyday. Several of us got together and we started praying. There were some situations that changed, and things started improving. It was a slow change, but things did get better. All of a sudden, we noticed the Holy Spirit was back among us in worship. We could once again praise God with some freedom. We could see and feel the Holy Spirit moving again in our congregation. As we began to experience the freedom to worship, the devil was not a happy camper. He began once again to start his spiritual warfare on the church. He began to stir things up. He began to put doubts in people's minds and began to cause havoc. Several of us realized what was happening again. We counter-attacked with prayer and praise. So be aware, it may not only happen in your life, but it might happen in your church or Bible study group, as well.

How do we fight spiritual warfare? For me, it was a matter of realizing that the thoughts the devil was putting in my head were just that—the devil's thoughts, not mine and certainly not God's. How do I know that? God will never put thoughts in our minds that will degrade us or make us think badly about anyone else or ourselves. He would not put thoughts in us that would keep us from having the freedom to worship. God wants us to think good thoughts.

After realizing that, the next step was to call upon God to help fight the battle. That is exactly what I did. I prayed and prayed. God called me to put on the armor of God—faith, truth, righteousness, the hope of salvation, and the Word of God—and I did just that. God

SPIRITUAL WARFARE

wasn't going to let me fight the battle alone, and He wouldn't fight the battle without me. We won! The devil decided to lay low for a while. Will he return? Sure he will. The great thing is I now know I can fight him and with God's help, I can win. I have experienced spiritual warfare and won! Wow, if that isn't a wonderful feeling.

I believe that if we never experience spiritual warfare we should be concerned. It is only as we grow closer to God and upset the devil that we experience it. If we aren't working for God, the devil isn't concerned about us. It is when we are actively working for God that causes the devil to get upset with us. It is something that makes us grow stronger in our Christian walk.

Ephesians 6:10-11 says, "A final word: Be strong in the Lord and in his mighty power. Put on all of God's armor so that you will be able to stand firm against all strategies of the devil." If you are experiencing spiritual warfare, put on the armor of God and be ready to fight. If you aren't experiencing spiritual warfare or never have, then maybe you should reevaluate your Christian walk. It could be you are not a threat to the devil. Could it be a time for you to start moving forward again? Looking back, it is kind of fun fighting the devil and winning. With Christ on our side, we will always be on the winning side. Don't try to fight the devil without God. It won't work. We are not strong enough. We need God to help protect us and shield us from evil thoughts. Next time the devil is warring against you, put the full armor of God on and watch the devil flee.

> "A final word: Be strong in the Lord and in his mighty power. Put on all of God's armor so that you will be able to stand firm against all strategies of the devil. For we are not fighting against flesh-and-blood enemies, but against evil rulers and authorities of the unseen world, against mighty powers in this dark world, and against evil spirits in the heavenly places. Therefore, put on every piece of God's armor so you will be able to resist the enemy in the time of evil. Then after the battle you will still be standing firm."
>
> *Ephesians 6:10-13*

◄ **L.T. FROG**

Prayer: Dear gracious Father, I know the devil will try all kinds of tricks to pull me over to his side. He will lie, put evil thoughts in my mind, and even make bad things look good. He will attack my family and friends. He will use them against me. Thank you for giving me armor to put on for protection. Thank you that I do not have to fight the war against the devil alone. I know that all I have to do is call out to you and you will be there with me. Help me to remain strong in you and resist the devil's temptations. I give you praise as I win the battle over Satan and watch him flee. Amen.

Stages of Life

Luke 15:11-31

As I get older, I realize every stage of life is a new learning process. I learn something new about myself. A new idea has been revealed, an old thought has a different perspective, and if I allow myself, I can learn at every stage.

For me now, the new stage I have entered is having young adult children who can and will make up their own minds and do the things they think are best for them. It is hard as a parent not to step in as I did when they were younger and tell them what they can and can't do or what is best for them. Sometimes they ask for advice and sometimes they take my advice—other times they don't and that is okay, too. Their lives belong to them, and even though it is hard to step aside and see them work through their problems and challenges, they must experience life for themselves. That is when they will grow and become stronger.

Now, I am sure my parents are laughing at me. I know I always challenged them. I know Greg, my husband, and I did things my parents and his parents were not in favor of and did not approve of. We made mistakes and we learned from our mistakes. They still loved and helped us. So it is with our own children. They are bound to make mistakes, and we will be there when they do to pick them up and love them just the same.

I know God must feel the same way about me today. I know as an adult I still make mistakes and do some things He doesn't like. I make decisions sometimes without even asking for guidance from Him. Sometimes I make mistakes and then wish I had asked for His guidance. Most of the time when I mess things up, I can go before Him, ask for forgiveness, and ask for His help to straighten things out. Sometimes I ask for His guidance and still make the decision to do what I want to do. Which is silly; why waste His time asking if I am going to be bull-headed and do things my way?

The important thing is just like we are with our children, He is always there waiting for us to come back to Him and acknowledge that we goofed. I punish myself worse than He ever would, most of the time. He never leaves me or forsakes me no matter how much I mess things up. We would never leave our kids hanging. As long as we are able, we will help them. He is there just to love, to forgive and to accept me just as I am—a Christian living in a worldly world.

In the Bible story of the Prodigal Son, the son wants his inheritance now, not in the future. He wants to do things his way. I am sure you could add to this and figure out that working on the family farm was not his idea of a "wonderful life." A wonderful life was out "there" waiting for him. Instead of asking Dad for his advice, he asked for his share of the inheritance. We all know what happens. He gets into the world and for a while he is living a "wonderful life." Suddenly something happens—the money is gone. He has no job, no education, and no where to turn. He can't face going home to his father as a failure, so he tries to make it on his own. He ends up working on a farm (where he didn't want to be) feeding pigs. He was so hungry he longed to eat the same food the pigs were eating. He realized his father's hired hands were doing better than he. So, he swallowed his pride and returned home to ask for a job as a hired hand on the farm he left behind. The father, being so excited to see his son is still alive, welcomes him back and they have a wonderful celebration. All is well with the son once more.

It is the same with us. We know what is best for us. We demand the best of everything now. We don't want to wait. God's timing is too slow. We are in too big a hurry. We do things our way. We often find we have messed up and things aren't turning out as planned. We can't call on God. We can't swallow our pride so we try as hard as we can to straighten things out our own way. More times than not, we just get in deeper and deeper. I have been there, done that, and don't want to do it again. Every time I have messed up, God has been there just like the father was, waiting for me to come home. All I had to do was swallow my pride, ask for forgiveness and accept His love. It is not easy, but that's what God wants from us. None of us would turn our backs on our children. We love them unconditionally. We love them no matter how bad things get.

It is the same with our Heavenly Father. He is waiting to welcome us back. Which stage are you in? Are you the child hating to swallow your pride and go home? Or are you the parent waiting to extend unconditional love toward your child? If you are the child, I pray that today you will swallow your pride and go home. You will be welcomed with open arms. If you are the parent, I pray as your child comes home you will forgive and forget. God has forgiven us and loves us; it is only right that we do that towards others.

> *"But his father said to the servants, 'Quick! Bring the finest robe in the house and put it on him. Get a ring for his finger and sandals for his feet. And kill the calf we have been fattening. We must celebrate with a feast, for this son of mine was dead and has now returned to life. He was lost, but now he is found.' So the party began."*
>
> *Luke 15:22-24*

Prayer: Dear Jesus, it is not always easy to sit and watch my children make choices. I want to tell them how to live their lives; I don't want them to suffer from making mistakes. I know that the only way I learn and grow is through my mistakes. It is not easy to swallow my pride and admit my mistakes because I am afraid of being turned away. Thank you, God, because I know you are always there to welcome me back and to love me. You are waiting with open arms. Thank you for who you are and for what you do for me. Amen.

The Cross and the Electric Chair

John 3:16

There is a chorus we sing that says, "I stand amazed in all of your glory, that you would die for me!" The truth is that I am amazed He died for me. I am just an ordinary person, nothing special, yet He died for me! When He was on the cross, He saw me. Pretty powerful stuff, huh?

One Easter, I was given the task of delivering the Sunrise Service. My text that morning was John 3:16. We all know the text so well. We can repeat it as well as we can repeat our own name. *"For God loved the world so much that he gave his one and only Son, so that everyone who believes in him will not perish but have eternal life."* Do we understand the true meaning of that text?

Let me put it in layman's terms. God gave His only Son to die for our sins. All we have to do is believe in Him. He had one Son, whom he sacrificed for us. We all have someone special in our lives; a son or a daughter, even a husband or wife. If not, we have someone else who is special to us; a friend or an extended relative. Think about that someone special for just a minute. Think about what makes them special. Picture their face in your mind. Today, when we punish someone for their sins we no longer hang them on a cross. Instead, in some states, we use the "electric chair." Now, would you allow that someone special in your life to be strapped (sacrificed) in an electric chair for your sins; for something you did? Or how about sacrificing that person for the prostitute who hangs out on the corners in your own town? Or those kids hanging on the street corner we detest so much? Or would you allow someone special to die in the electric chair for a neighbor or that relative you haven't spoken to in years because of a family squabble? Would you allow that person to die for your pastor?

That is exactly what Christ did. He took His only Son and allowed Him to die for you and me. I love all my church family and friends with the love of the Lord, but I would not put my daughters in the electric chair just so they could live forever. Especially, since they didn't do anything to deserve it. I don't have the power or the strength to do that. I don't have the ability to watch them die an undeserving death. You know what? I don't have to and neither do you. It has already been done for us.

God has already allowed His Son to die for each of us; also, for those I mentioned above—the prostitute or those kids hanging loose, or the drug addicts, or anyone else you can think of who does not deserve eternal life.

Those people that we think are undeserving may not know that Christ has died for them. If they know, they may not care. However, the fact remains Christ has died on the cross for all of us! Not just the chosen ones, but for all of us; no matter where we stand in this life. It is only those who believe who will be saved and have eternal life.

Another aspect of this is God turning His back and closing His ears on His Son when He called out to Him. When Christ cried out, God closed His ears for a few minutes. He turned His back on His Son. Once your special person is strapped in and cries out for you, could you turn your back and not try to help in some way? I wouldn't even be able to watch the death of my child, and then to hear Him cry out in agony; that would be too much for me to bear. I would be crushed and broken and so would you. None of us have the power or strength to go through that. None of us deserves what Christ has

THE CROSS AND THE ELECTRIC CHAIR

done for us, but that didn't make a difference to God. He allowed it to happen to His only Son. He does not ask us to do this. Only He has the power and strength to do something like this just so you and I can live with Him eternally. All we have to do is believe. He did it so that those who believe in God, those who are obedient and live out their lives in His Word and truth, may live forever. We will never experience death. Our earthly bodies will, but we will not. How awesome is that?

The next time you read John 3:16 remember what God did for us. Stop and ask yourself could I do what God did? Take a minute and offer praises to God for sending His only begotten Son to die on the cross for you so you can live with Him forever. I pray the next time you read John 3:16 it comes alive for you. It has for me.

"For God loved the world so much that he gave his one and only Son, so that everyone who believes in him will not perish but have eternal life."

John 3:16

Prayer: Dear God, I can't even begin to thank you for what you did. I am not a deserving person, yet you sacrificed your only Son for me. You did it so that I may have life eternally and live with you. You don't ask for much in return. You just ask me to believe in you, to trust you with my life, and to be obedient to your Word. What an awesome Father. Help me in my unbelief and in my trust as I try to be obedient. Thank you for sending your Son to die for my sins. I give you praise, glory, and honor for all you do. Amen.

Use All Your Strength — Including Your Father's

I John 5:14-15

I once heard a story about a boy and his father who were taking a walk along a road. They came across a huge stone. The little boy asked his dad, "Do you think I could move the stone using all my strength?" The dad told the boy he *did* think he could move the stone if he used all his strength. Well, the boy reached down and tried moving the stone. He pushed and he pushed. He pushed so long and so hard and yet the stone didn't move at all. He finally grew tired and gave up. He turned to his dad and told him that he was wrong. He used all his strength and couldn't move the stone. The father lovingly told his son that he didn't use all the strength available to him. The boy looked at his dad. The dad reached around behind the boy and put his arms under his son's arms and together they pushed the stone.

Well, isn't that typical of the human race? How many times have we tried to do something on our own without asking for our Father's help or advice? How many times have we tried, tried, and tried to do something on our own without seeking advice or help from others? We don't want to admit that we can't do it on our own. To admit we can't do some things on our own might suggest we are weak or not smart enough to figure it out. Often times we fail and have to give up or ask for help from our parents. By that time, things are a mess. Wouldn't it be so much easier to ask for help the first time? How much quicker could we get our work done if we just ask for a little help? Many times there are obstacles in our way, and we try to move them without any help.

Our Father is just waiting to hear us ask for help. In I John 5:14-15, it says:

"And we are confident that he hears us whenever we ask for anything that pleases him. And since we know he hears us when we make our requests, we also know that he will give us what we ask for."

All we have to do is ask Him for strength, wisdom, and knowledge and we can accomplish all things great and small. We often make a mountain out of a mole hill, yet we know God can move mountains.

There have been numerous times I have tried to accomplish tasks without asking for His guidance and failed. Every time I write my articles or devotions and don't ask for His guidance, I fail. When I was speaking on Wednesday evenings, I sometimes would deliver my devotions with my own strength and would fail. When I ask God to use me, and I allow Him to come and fill me with His strength, I manage to give a good devotion. Anyone can do anything they want to accomplish as long as they ask God to guide them, give them strength, and then let God fill them with His strength. My favorite verse is, *"For I can do everything through Christ, who gives me strength"* (Philippians 4:13). I have used this many times when trying to accomplish a difficult task, no matter what that task is.

During one particular difficult time in our lives, we had to go on food stamps. My husband had lost his job and was going to school to get some training. We had three small daughters who depended on us, and I wasn't working at the time. My husband went with me to apply for the assistance. When it came to picking them up on a monthly basis, that was my job. I would have to go to the courthouse

USE ALL YOUR STRENGTH – INCLUDING YOUR FATHER'S

and pick them up. I was embarrassed about it, and that was the last thing I wanted to do. People are not very sensitive to other's feelings when it comes to something like this. I was not always treated very nice when it came to me spending them at the grocery store. Stares and looks of disgust were on most people's faces that I encountered. It was a very humbling experience. The only way I managed to get through those times was by asking God to help me move those mountains and give me strength. I needed His help as I went to pick up the stamp and go to the grocery store. This experience taught me to be very tolerant of other people's needs. I am much more sensitive to those needing food stamps now. I walked in another person's shoes for a while and experienced how they were treated. I also became very dependent on God. Our Father is waiting to be heard. Do you have a task that needs accomplishing? He is more than ready to help you move mountains, give you strength, and share a bit of wisdom with you. All you have to do is ask and believe.

"'You don't have enough faith,' Jesus told them. 'I tell you the truth, if you had faith even as small as a mustard seed, you could say to this mountain, 'Move from here to there,' and it would move. Nothing would be impossible.'"

Matthew 17:20-21

Prayer: Dear God, I think I can do all things using my own strength, but often times I fail. I am a proud person and don't like asking for help. Throughout the Bible, you have given me examples of people who have asked for help: Moses counted on his brother to help him; the disciples counted on each other. I am no different. I need help to see a clear path as I make decisions about my life. I need strength to move mountains. I ask, God, for you to take away my pride and help me seek you. I thank you for always being there for me. Amen.

Peace

John 14:27

Peace. Everyone wants it, but what is it? What is your definition of peace? Is the peace you understand different than God's peace that He gives? Let's examine the definition of peace.

First, in your own mind, define peace. Is it the quiet times when the kids aren't fighting or arguing? Or the times when you aren't debating with your spouse over some minor imperfections in each other's personalities? Do you define peace as those times when countries are actually getting along and there is no rumor of war? Is peace defined, in your terms, as contentment?

Webster's dictionary defines peace as "freedom from war, an agreement to end war, law and order, harmony, serenity, calm, or quiet." That's a good definition of peace, but it's not the peace I want to talk about right now. The peace that I want to talk about is the kind God gives as we turn our lives over to Him. I believe that is a different kind of peace. I have experienced God's peace. It is more than just having freedom from war; it is more than law and order. It's a peace that passes all understanding.

The Smith's Bible Dictionary describes peace this way: "quiet, ease, security." It goes on to say, "Peace unto you was a common form of Eastern salutation, peace as the opposite of war." Those are still good definitions of peace. However, that's still not the definition of peace I am talking about. The definition of peace that I am defining is beyond understanding. It is something you just can't understand unless you experience it firsthand.

There is a difference between the peace the world can give us and the peace God gives us. In John 14:27, Jesus says, *"I am leaving you with a gift—peace of mind and heart. And the peace I give is a gift the world cannot give. So don't be troubled or afraid."* We can be at peace in this world and still not know what true peace is. Everything around us could be going smoothly, yet we still feel unsettled. We still do not have that inner peace we long for.

Romans 5:1 says, *"Therefore, since we have been made right in God's sight by faith, we have peace with God because of what Jesus Christ our Lord has done for us."* If we have accepted God and have faith, then we receive God's peace. Not the peace the world gives, but God's peace. How do I explain God's peace? For me, peace is when the world tumbles down all around me, and I'm okay. When everything in my life seems chaotic, I still have a sense that everything is going to be okay. There have been times in my life when my world was falling apart, everyone around me was fretting and worrying, but I had a sense of serenity or an unexplained peace. Some looked at me like I was nuts. They had seen me in the past fretting, worrying, and stewing with them and now I was the calm one. What had happened, they wondered. Some even asked me to explain my actions. It was simple. Most knew I was a Christian already. It was when I began to let God control my life that He sent His peace. When I decided to give up control of things that I had no control over and let God have complete control of my life, was when I first experienced "real" peace. I have a saying in my office that goes, "Maybe part of trusting God is coming to the place where you realize there is nothing you can do for yourself anymore." I had come to that place. I realized that nothing I could do could change the situation. I had to give God complete trust, faith, and control.

It's hard to explain. That's why it is called peace that passes all understanding. Unless, you've been there, you just can't explain

PEACE

it. One summer when we went to Florida, a few times I'd get up before anyone else and walk to the beach. There were benches there. I'd sit on the bench just staring at the water and the sky. No one else was around and I was lost in the surroundings. That comes close to describing the peace that God gives me. Another way I can explain the peace for me is through a picture I was given for Christmas one year from my Wednesday morning Bible study class. I had taught Bible study, and the members knew one of my favorite stories was Peter walking on the water. The picture I have is of Christ walking on water. Around Christ's head is a yellow glow. Christ is looking down on the water. His face has one of the most peaceful looks I have seen. Every time I look at the face of Christ, I see the peace He offers me as I begin to step out of the boat and walk on the water. When I begin to experience a little of that peace, I find I always want more of it. If you see a beautiful sunset and you get lost in the moment and you feel a sense of peace and serenity, that's it, only better!

Unfortunately, I am human and I don't always experience the peace that God wants to give me. Why? Romans 8:6 explains this: *"The mind of sinful man is death, but the mind controlled by the Spirit is life and peace."* Verse 8 says, *"Those controlled by the sinful nature cannot please God."* There are those times I do take my eyes off of Christ. There are times I get too busy and don't read my Bible, pray, or work on my faith. I let my mind drift away from God. Those are the times I get caught up in my surroundings. I let those around me affect me, and I let life's troubles get me down. It's then that I lose the peace I long for and want. What do I do then? I go back and get on my knees and ask God to take over control of my life once again. I set my eyes on Christ and the path He leads me down. I have to readjust my focus on Christ. Then, once again, I experience the peace that passes all understanding.

In Romans 14:19 it says, *"So then, let us aim for harmony in the church and try to build each other up."* We ourselves have to make the effort to keep our minds focused on Christ. Once we keep our minds focused, we can begin to put our faith and trust in God and then comes the peace. It is an action we have to take. My husband can often be challenging. Someone once asked me the secret to being married to Greg. My answer was no secret. You have to work at a marriage twenty-four hours a day, seven days a week, all 365 days a year. Once you begin to ease up, your marriage can fall into trouble. That is the way it is with your faith. You have to work at it. It is a constant thing. Once we have learned to put our faith and trust in God we give Him control of our lives, and He will send us His peace.

Philippians 4:7 says, *"Then you will experience God's peace, which exceeds anything we can understand. His peace will guard your hearts and minds as you live in Christ Jesus."* Once we have experienced this peace, we can then become peaceful about every situation God puts us in. We won't let circumstances or people control our thoughts and behavior. The more we experience this kind of peace, the more we want. It is not easy to obtain. It's a matter of giving up control of your life, trusting God in all situations, and having faith that He will be with you to the end.

I hope your definition of peace has changed. I hope each of you are longing for just this kind of peace. I wish for each of you the peace that God gives, the peace that passes all understanding. If you don't have this kind of peace today, I ask that you will consider giving up control of your life and let God take over. Start today trusting and having faith in God. Realize that there is nothing you can do for yourself anymore to help with the situation. Give it to God and then experience a new kind of peace. One that only God gives, not the kind the world gives.

> *"Then you will experience God's peace, which exceeds anything we can understand. His peace will guard your hearts and minds as you live in Christ Jesus."*
>
> *Philippians 4:7*

Prayer: Dear Lord, I thank you for peace. I want the peace that you offer and not the world. The world's peace is not authentic. Your peace is a real, soul satisfying peace, one the world can't understand. I want your peace; the peace that the world truly does not know or understand. Thank you, Lord, for the peace I experience as I go through life trusting in you. I give you all the praise and glory for those times I have peace in my life. Amen.

I Did It Again!

Romans 7:7-25

Well, I did it again. Just about once a year I do it. It frustrates me. I try so hard to keep from doing it, too! But I did it. I knew it was wrong, but I just couldn't stop myself, and I get angry at myself every time. What did I do that was so wrong? What is it that I do about once a year? I take my eyes off Jesus and allow myself to get caught up in things, in circumstances around me, and I let people distract me. I lost my focus. I could blame it on things, I could blame it on the circumstances, and I could even put the blame on people around me (and I probably did at one time). But the truth of the matter is, it's no one's fault but my own. That is what makes me angry. You'd think year after year I'd learn. But, I don't. I am only human, and I mess up.

At one point, I even prayed God would remove me from what was going on around me. I prayed that God would change the circumstance; I prayed and prayed and prayed. I never seemed to be getting anywhere. I didn't get any answers, I didn't get removed from the situation, nothing happened. Then one day I was reading my morning devotion and it hit me like a ton of bricks. I had gotten caught up in my surroundings and took my focus off God and the cross. I was allowing people to distract me with their grumblings about how hard life is and how unfair life can be at times. I started focusing on circumstances that were taking place in my life. I took my focus off God.

Once I realized what had happened, I knew immediately what I needed to do (mainly because I have been at this place before). I had to get down and pray a prayer of forgiveness. I had to start focusing on my Savior, my Redeemer, and my God once again. I had to ignore those things that were going on around me and let God have control. I had to do whatever it took to get back on the right track again. Once again, I switched my focus to God and the cross. Once again I was feeling better and stronger. I had a renewed determination to not let anyone or anything take my eyes off God again (although I know it will happen again because I am human).

Why am I telling you about my sin? Why am I telling you about my faults and my shortcomings? Because Satan likes to do anything he can to cause trouble, and we have to be ready for him. When we realize we have taken our eyes off of God, and we get into that worldly mind set, that is when Satan comes along and attacks us. He'll attack us anywhere and by any means. He'll use our friends, our church, our family, and yes, any circumstance he can to make sure we are focused on him and not his favorite enemy, God.

So how do we counterattack? The answer is simple: by putting on the armor of God found in Ephesians 6:10-11: *"A final word: Be strong in the Lord and in his mighty power. Put on all of God's armor so that you will be able to stand firm against all strategies of the devil."* I like verse 18 found in the same chapter, too: *"Pray in the Spirit at all times and on every occasion. Stay alert and be persistent in your prayers for all believers everywhere."*

When Satan comes a-knocking we need to be praying. We need to pray for the person or circumstance Satan is using to try to distract us, we need to pray for power and strength to confess God before men, and we need to take a stand. I don't mean taking a stand on the circumstances, taking sides (like people would like), or even giving your opinion; instead we need to stand up for God. We need to stop the devil right in his tracks and say, "Enough is enough. I am no longer going to allow the devil to distract me from doing God's will." Satan will even convince you that you don't know God's will (just like he did me). God's will for our lives is simple. God's will is for us to live so God's light can shine through us. God's light can't shine through us if we allow Satan to stand in the middle.

I have fought the battle of spiritual warfare, and I have come out a little bruised, sore, and worn out. But, I have won, and I am stronger! I am refocused on God and am taking a stand as of today. I will no longer allow circumstances (in church, at home, or anywhere else for that matter), people (family, friends, enemies, or others), or anything to take my eyes off God. I know what I must do, and I plan on doing it stronger than ever.

Won't you join me in my stand? Together, let's defeat Satan and once again allow God to move in our midst. Let us all refocus on God and not on circumstances, events, or people. It is only through God we can once again have peace that passes all understanding and allow God to have the freedom He desires in our hearts, our lives and yes, even in our worship.

Join me today.

"So the trouble is not with the law, for it is spiritual and good. The trouble is with me, for I am all too human, a slave to sin. I don't really understand myself, for I want to do what is right, but I don't do it. Instead, I do what I hate. But if I know that what I am doing is wrong, this shows that I agree that the law is good. So I am not the one doing wrong; it is sin living in me that does it. And I know that nothing good lives in me, that is, in my sinful nature. I want to do what is right, but I can't. I want to do what is good, but I don't. I don't want to do what is wrong, but I do it anyway. But if I do what I don't want to do, I am not really the one doing wrong; it is sin living in me that does it."

Romans 7:14-20

L.T. FROG

Prayer: Dear God, I don't like to sin. I do things I don't want to do. I often get caught up in circumstances around me. I take my eyes off you. Sometimes it is a constant battle to do good and do what is right. I am human; I fail in my walk with you. I know I am going to mess up. Thank you for providing a way to restore my relationship with you. I know when I mess up all I have to do is come before you and confess my sins and ask for forgiveness. You sent your Son to Earth to die for my sins. Thank you that He died for all my sins. Let me now come before you and confess my sins and ask for forgiveness. You have forgiven me, so now let me forget my past sin and move on to do what is good and right. I ask all these things in thy name. Amen.

Spiritual Therapy: How's Yours?

James 5:16

After having surgery, my husband had to spend several months in physical therapy. We went twice a week. The therapist worked with him on gaining control of the muscles in his shoulder. They also worked with him on gaining strength. It was very intense. Sometimes he would come home with more pain than when he went in. They kept telling him no pain, no gain. At home we would have exercises to do. I pushed him to do his exercises and then there were exercises he and I had to do together. I have often laughed and said, "If a husband and wife can survive physical therapy together, they can survive anything."

One day after coming home from therapy, I began to think about how each of us could use some therapy. I am not necessarily talking about physical therapy, but spiritual therapy. In order for Greg to be stronger and better he had to be disciplined. He also had a therapist that helped, taught, and pushed him. It makes sense to me that if we want to be better and stronger Christians, we need to be disciplined. We need to make it a practice every day to do some sort of Christian exercise. It may be reading the Bible the first thing in the morning and the last thing at night. It may be spending time in prayer. It may be spending time visiting shut-ins or nursing home patients or even people in the hospital. Another exercise we could practice would be to share our faith with others on a daily basis. We need to get in the habit of exercising our faith. Not just once in awhile, but every day. Jesus exercised His faith every day as He traveled from village to village preaching the good news.

Twice a week, Greg had to "go" to physical therapy and do extra work there. It also makes sense to me that as Christians, we need to "go" and get some extra therapy. For some it may mean going to church on Sunday or a midweek service, going to a Bible study, and then once or twice a year going on a Christian retreat. Whatever we decide, we need that extra boost to help us get better and stronger. When my husband went to physical therapy, he was held accountable for those daily exercises. They knew if he had been doing them or not. If he hadn't, it showed because there would not have been any improvement or very little. If he did them daily, they could see improvement when he went. It also told them he was trying to improve and do his best. They encouraged him and even divulged that they were proud of his hard work.

When we attend church, we are held accountable for our daily exercises. It shows if we are not doing them. I have noticed people sitting for several minutes trying to find a book in the Bible. It tells me they have not read the Bible enough, or studied the Bible enough to become familiar with it. It looks foreign to them. I have seen people who have been in church for years, but their actions tell me they don't practice what they have heard on Sunday morning. They don't practice their exercises. They are under the impression that Sunday morning is enough. You have to be disciplined to do your "Christian exercise" daily or you will never be stronger or better. You have to make it a practice to "go" to therapy on a regular basis, and more than once a week is an advantage to improving your faith.

Sometimes my husband would come home in pain. It took a few hours or days for the soreness to go away. Again, we must remember no pain, no gain. It is the same way with being a Christian. Sometimes it hurts and there is pain involved. Sometimes we don't want to hear what the minister is telling us. Or maybe God is telling us something

SPIRITUAL THERAPY: HOW'S YOURS?

and we have to face the truth, but the truth hurts. As I have said before we can't have our mountaintops if we don't experience the valleys. Sometimes when we grow stronger and better in our faith, it hurts. We have to change something in our personality, and sometimes we have to learn to forgive, when all we want is to never forgive. Our toes may be stepped on, our hearts broken. Yet, after a few hours or days (and sometimes months) we find we are stronger and better. We even hate to admit it, but we have reached the short-term goal we have aimed for. We are stretching and gaining control. We are getting stronger and better.

When Greg arrived at therapy, there was a therapist waiting for him. She pushed, she tugged, and she stretched his muscles. She inquired about how his daily therapy was going. She asked questions about the pain. She went the extra mile in helping him rebuild those muscles, tendons, and biceps he'd lost. We can and should use God as our therapist. God should be there to guide, direct, and lead us. There is another kind of therapist I think we all need to consider. We need to see about investing our time with a Christian therapist. Who, you ask would that be? A friend, Bible study partner, or prayer partner would make an excellent therapist. A relative would be good, also. It needs to be someone who will push you, who tugs at you, and someone who will stretch your mind. Someone who will take a few minutes each week from his or her life and ask how you are doing. Someone who wants to know how your daily exercise is coming along. We need a therapist who will be there when we experience pain. We need to share our pain. We need to let him or her know we hurt. We need someone who will go the extra mile for us, someone who will help us grow stronger and better.

Greg helped the physical therapist in return. He helped her as she helped him. That's the way it should be with us, too. We need to be a spiritual therapist for others. There may be one person you know that you would like to team up with. You would like to see them be a stronger and better Christian. You feel you could help that person accomplish their goal of being more Christ-like. It could be that you may be a spiritual therapist for one person and another person will be your spiritual therapist. They could be two different people. However it works out, find your therapist and start working together on getting stronger and better.

Becoming a stronger and better Christian is pretty simple if you think about it. It is a simple routine. Exercise daily, go to your place of Christian therapy, and have your own Christian therapist help you along the way. We spend hours exercising our physical bodies and getting them in shape so we may be stronger and better. Isn't it time we spend hours on our spiritual bodies so we can get them in shape and be stronger?

Let's get out there and start doing our exercises! Let's be stronger and better Christians. God bless.

> *"Two people are better off than one, for they can help each other succeed. If one person falls, the other can reach out and help. But someone who falls alone is in real trouble."*
>
> *Ecclesiastes 4:9-10*

Prayer: Dear God, I don't like to exercise my body, much less my mind. I find time for other things I like to do, but I say I can't find time to read your Word, pray, or even attend church. I know in my heart that exercise is good for me. Help me as I begin to exercise my faith more, sharing with one another in word and deed. I need to hold others accountable; help me find that special someone who will hold me accountable. If there is no one then I ask you, dear Lord, to hold me accountable for my actions. Teach me daily to be more like you in all my ways. I ask all these things in thy name. Amen.

Who Will Be Your "Stitcher" for the Year?

Psalm 119:105-109, Psalm 86:11-12

I love to sit and cross stitch. I enjoy doing that along with some other hobbies I have recently acquired. It always fascinates me each time I start a project. When I start a cross-stitch project, I begin with a piece of Aida cloth. There is nothing on it. It is blank, just like the calendar year. I start with one stitch and then another and another. I can't seem to wait until the picture begins to form on the cloth. Even though I know what the picture is supposed to look like, I still get eager to see it come into reality. There are times I may make mistakes and have to take stitches out and redo them, or I get lost and have to figure out where I am. Once I have fixed my mistake or found out where I am, I am on my way again, and, once again, the excitement settles in. I finish the picture and am amazed at how it turns out. Even though I know from an example how it is supposed to look, I am still amazed.

At the start of each New Year our calendar is blank. Usually, we have set goals and some things we'd like to see get accomplished during the year. Maybe some dates have already been filled in for us. There might be some vacations planned, new grandchildren coming, and a new job to learn, moves that have to be made. Maybe we have some commitments that are a holdover from last year. Whatever the case may be, we have a new year to anticipate and to get excited. There is no use looking back over last year. It is gone; we can't get it back, and we can't change what happened to us in the past year. But, we can learn from our failures as well as our successes. As we start each new day, it is like a new stitch. At the end of the year, we will have a picture of what this year was like. For some, it may not be a pretty picture while for others, those who allow God to work them, a beautiful picture can be created. We may make some mistakes throughout the year, and we may lose our way sometimes, but as long as we find our way back and ask God to forgive us for those mistakes we have made, it doesn't matter. What is important is allowing our "pattern" to be the Bible and the "stitcher" to be God. If we allow God to move in us and through us, our lives can become a beautiful reflection of what God wants us to be.

When I am done cross stitching, most of the time, I have to do some outlining. When you outline something, it adds the finishing touch to your project. It just makes it look a little nicer. Sometimes outlining isn't easy. Sometimes during the year, God adds that finishing touch to us. Sometimes that finishing touch can be a little rough. It can be hard to get through it, but if we make it through those rough times, we can always look back and see how much beauty it added to our picture. Sometimes outlining can be easy. God gives us plenty of grace and mercy throughout the year. He blesses us so much with health, wealth, family, and friends. He just adds that finishing touch in our lives in so many different ways.

At the end of the year, we can look back at our "picture" (the year) and set it aside. We can look back on the picture but we can never redo it. We can't make changes, we can't go back and take out stitches and add new ones. All we can do is to start all over the following year, with a new blank piece of material (or a new year), and allow God once again to be the stitcher and our pattern to be the Bible. Instead of trying to be the stitcher ourselves, we need to give God complete control and allow Him to work through us. Sometimes when we try to help God, we just get in His way and our

WHO WILL BE YOUR "STITCHER" FOR THE YEAR?

beautiful picture turns out all wrong. That is when we have to take the stitches out and let God rework our lives to fit His pattern for us. This next year, I hope you will allow God to be the "stitcher" of your life. My wish for each of you is that you take the time to read the Bible, make it your pattern and then allow God to work through you, so at the end of the year God can look at His picture and say, "How beautiful!"

God Bless each of you and your families!

"Trust in the Lord with all your heart; do not depend on your own understanding. Seek His will in all you do, and He will show you which path to take."

Proverbs 3:5-6

Prayer: Dear God, I thank you for being my stitcher. I give you my life, asking you to be in control. Life is not easy, and I am not sure what I am to be doing or what it's all about. Because I am called your daughter (son) in Christ, I can trust you to lead me and guide me in the direction you would have me go. Thank you for giving me each new year to explore, to be challenged, to grow, and to stretch. Help me to take each year and live it more fully for you. Amen.

God's Blessing

Matthew 5:4, 6; Romans 8:28

October 10, 1999, was a very special day for us. On that day twenty-one years before, our beautiful baby boy was born. He was truly a blessing. He was also a gift from Heaven. Because my husband is an outdoorsman, I wanted a son for him; someone who could hunt, fish, and do all those guy things. This was truly an answer to my prayers. Now I wouldn't be stuck going to gun shows, hunting, or listening for hours about all those things men talk about with their sons. Six weeks after his birth, our son passed away. We were heartbroken. Greg would later find out he'd have to settle for having three daughters. That was not a bad thing. We have three beautiful daughters who have blessed us over the years in so many ways.

After looking back, although I miss our son deeply, I am grateful for the events surrounding his death. I might not be where I am today if things had turned out differently. It was because of our son's death and many other events in our lives that have led me to live the life I now lead. It was only through much suffering and anguish that I have become stronger in Christ. It is true that trials and temptations lead to a stronger relationship with Christ. I might have become like so many others today and put God on the backburner and saved Him for when I got older and more "settled."

I often wonder what kind of son we might have had; what would he have grown up to be? Would he have played sports, been in the band, an honor student, or would he have caused us much trouble? Only God knows the answer to those questions. Only God saw the future. We donated his eyes when he passed away. Due to the many medicines he had been on that were trying to save his life, his eyes were the only thing that could be used. I think God knew someone could benefit from his eyes. Like a pastor once told me, "Life is not fair, but God knows what He is doing." We can't see the whole picture. My mom once told me that life is like a football game. We can see only one play at a time, but God is in the stands and can see the whole game. He even knows how it will end for each of us.

Twenty-one years later on October 9, 1999, God blessed Greg and I again with a son-in-law. God took one son and gave us another. This son hunts, fishes, collects guns, and does all those "guy" things. Greg and Shane talk for hours about things I have never been able to talk to Greg about. Shane understands those things Greg wishes I understood. It is wonderful seeing a new relationship form between father and son-in-law. I am amazed at how much they are alike. They go off for hours watching videos on hunting and guns. They laugh, talk, and share with each other for hours.

God has been good to Greg and me. After all these years, He is still blessing us. What a blessing we receive each time we think back to 1978 and reflect on those six weeks with our son. We were so proud of our newborn son. The happiness of having a son was overwhelming. In 1999, we found that happiness once again in having a son. This son, too, will make us proud as he strives to make a home for our daughter and himself. We cherished the relationship we had with our son for those brief six weeks. We have cherished the relationship we have had and will continue to have with our son-in-law. We only have God to thank for both of those relationships; it is only through Him those relationships were formed.

It is only when we get through things that we often see the blessings. I could never see how God had blessed me when my son died. How was losing him going to be a blessing? You

GOD'S BLESSING

may not see your blessing right away. It took several years for me to be able to say, "I see." It didn't hurt any less, but at the same time, I saw the whole picture. For me, the blessing was the strength to get through trials and tribulations. Since his death, I have had to call upon that strength many times. I have used that experience many times to help others in their Christian walks. Just recently, our granddaughter was born eight weeks prematurely. She, like our son, was in NICU, which is the Neonatal Intensive Care Unit. I was able to be with my daughter and calm her fears as together we went through this difficult time. I was able to help her understand some of the machines and their purpose for Allie. I was able to help Angie, my daughter, get through this. While we were going through this, I was able to reconnect with one of the nurses that had taken care of our son. What a blessing it was to be able to talk with someone who knew our son.

Have you gone through trials? Have you reflected lately on your blessings? Has God given you someone special in your life who you are thankful for? Have you told them how much you appreciate and love them?

As our sons and daughters begin a new life together with their mates, we need to be there for them, but at the same time not smother them. It is a difficult time for them. There are family traditions that will change and maybe even have to be broken. New traditions will replace the old ones. Families will be pulled and stretched as each young couple deals with the holidays. As Christian parents, it is our duty to love, support, and encourage them. We need to build them up, not tear them down.

I pray you will be as blessed in your relationships with your sons and daughters as we have been. As your children take spouses, I pray you will reach out in love and count them as part of your many blessings God has given you.

God bless each of the new relationships being formed in our lives.

L.T. FROG

"Dear friends, since God loved us that much, we surely ought to love each other."

I John 4:11

"And may the Lord make your love for one another and for all people grow and overflow, just as our love for you overflows."

I Thessalonians 3:12

Prayer: Dear Lord, I don't always understand what is happening to me. I don't like the things I go through, but it is through those difficult times that I grow in strength and knowledge. I learn not to lean on myself, but to lean on you. Thank you for always being there for me. I thank you also for those you bring into my life who bring me joy. Help me to remember to express my love and joy to them. It is better to build up than to tear down. Teach me how to build others up so your love will be seen in them. Thank you for all the blessings you bestow on me each day. Amen.

Worry? Who Me?

Philippians 4

> "Don't worry about anything; instead, pray about everything. Tell God what you need, and thank him for all he has done. Then you will experience God's peace, which exceeds anything we can understand. His peace will guard your hearts and minds as you live in Christ Jesus. . . Not that I was ever in need, for I have learned how to be content with whatever I have. I know how to live on almost nothing or with everything. I have learned the secret of living in every situation, whether it is with a full stomach or empty, with plenty or little. For I can do everything through Christ, who gives me strength."
>
> *Philippians 4:6-7, 11-13*

Isn't that a pretty powerful scripture? There are several issues to deal with in this small passage. The first statement is profound in itself. It says we are not to worry about anything. We are to pray and ask God for everything we need and then to give Him thanks. That means we are to hand over everything to God. Anything that causes us concern or worry, we should give to Him. There is nothing He can't handle and, believe me, after much experience I know He can handle things a lot better without our help. In fact, our prayers might get answered a lot quicker if we would leave well enough alone. That has been a hard lesson for me to learn (and one I am still learning). I want to give it to God and then think my job is stewing about it. According to Webster's dictionary, the meaning of "to stew" means to worry. So I haven't really given it over to God. I might like to think I have, but when it comes down to it, I haven't. Is there anything too small for God to handle? Is there anytime we should handle things instead of taking it to God? I don't think so. I think if it bothers us and we stew about it, then God is concerned about it, too.

Think back to the time when your kids were younger. Remember when they worried about something? Finally, after dragging it out of them, you realized it wasn't anything to fret over. After discussing the worry with them and coming up with some solutions, you both felt better. God loves us and calls us His children. There is nothing too small or too large for God. We are to give God everything that worries us. Anything that causes us to be anxious, troubled, annoyed, or uneasy, we are to take to God.

Part two of that same scripture reads "give thanks." Give Him thanks before we even get it? That's a strange idea isn't it? Well, if you read it correctly it says "always giving thanks." It doesn't say give thanks for giving us what we want. It just says to give thanks. We are to give God thanks for working in our lives and for listening to our prayers. If we are true Christians, we will allow God to answer our prayers the way He sees fit and the best way for us. Sometimes that might be yes, sometimes it might be no, or maybe, or not right now. I think God might even say to us, "Let me think about it for awhile, I want to ponder how I might best answer you." How many times as children did we go to our parents and they said, "Let me think about it for awhile"? I know there were times I had to wait for an answer. That's the way God is. We must be patient and wait for His answer. God will answer us, though not always according to our wishes. I try really hard to thank God for answering my prayers according to His wishes. That's what we must do. Thank Him for answering our prayers according to what He thinks is best for us. I have found that once I give God whatever it is that is worrying me, I thank Him for doing what is best for me.

The next part of the scripture comes alive. God's peace comes over me when I truly give it over to Him. It is really hard to describe the peace that overcomes me. It is a peace that passes all understanding. If you are a Christian then you know about that peace; you have experienced it. It's a calm assurance that all will be well because you know God loves you, and you have faith that He can be trusted to work all things for your good. It doesn't mean you won't have trials. But you know God will either remove the problem, or He will be right there with you, giving you whatever you need until the trials are over. In Joshua 1:5 God promises, *"I will never leave you nor forsake you."* The peace that comes to you makes you feel like the whole world has been lifted off of your shoulders. Once you have experienced it, you want more of it. The only way to gain more of this peace is to rely more fully on God, allowing Him to take over all of our burdens, no matter how big or how small they are. We can keep that peace by seeking God in prayer, reading and studying His Word, and relying on the Holy Spirit to guide us.

We shift gears a little bit in the next part. We need to learn to be content with how we are now. The next part says we need to be satisfied with the things we have and everything that happens. Once we give God our burdens and once we rely on God, He will take care of us. He will provide for us those things we need. Things or material possessions will not buy us happiness. Once we start accumulating things, then we want more things. We keep accumulating and accumulating until one day, we wake up and realize all of those things we have been accumulating haven't brought us any closer to happiness. We realize we still are not satisfied, and we wonder why. We must allow God to fill the void and satisfy our longing for worldly things. We can accumulate all we want, but when death comes knocking on our door, we go and our things are left behind for someone else. God will provide and we must be happy with the things He has provided for us. We also know (even if we don't want to admit it) everything happens for a reason. We don't always understand at the time it happens, but we have to realize there was a reason. Maybe the timing wasn't right, or it was going to turn out all wrong, or maybe there was a lesson to learn from it. We don't know, but if we trust God, then we must be satisfied with knowing God is in charge and everything will be okay. Read the Philippians 4:6-7, 11-13 text again:

> "Don't worry about anything; instead, pray about everything. Tell God what you need, and thank him for all he has done. Then you will experience God's peace, which exceeds anything we can understand. His peace will guard your hearts and minds as you live in Christ Jesus. . . Not that I was ever in need, for I have learned how to be content with whatever I have. I know how to live on almost nothing or with everything. I have learned the secret of living in every situation, whether it is with a full stomach or empty, with plenty or little. For I can do everything through Christ, who gives me strength."

This last part sums it all up. It doesn't matter how much or how little we have, the secret to Christian living is to be happy with how we are and who God created us to be. We are to be content with our surroundings whether we live in a palace or a hut. We are to fully rely on God no matter where He has placed us in life. He knows where He has placed us, He knows our way of life, and He knows everything about us there is to know. It is our choice to choose to honor him with our life and our possessions. It doesn't matter whether we have much or little; it's what we do with what He has given us that counts.

My favorite part: "For I can do everything through Christ, who gives me strength." I don't have to depend on my own strength to get me through this tough world. I don't have to depend on my own strength to get me through trials, tribulations, temptations, or anything else Satan throws at me. I can call on God to give me His strength, power, and might to get me through. I have used God's strength to get me through more times than I can count. Just like a poem says, God's strength has picked me up and carried me. When I saw only one set of footprints, it was because God was using His strength to carry me through the muck. Wow! Powerful stuff isn't it? Me, worry? Sure I will, because I am human and am still growing in Christ. But, I am growing to depend on Him more and more each day; and because of that I don't worry as much as I used to. How about you? Where are you in your walk? Keep this scripture close to you and when you begin to fret, pull it out and use it. God bless!

"I am leaving you with a gift—peace of mind and heart. And the peace I give is a gift the world cannot give. So don't be troubled or afraid."

John 14:27

Prayer: Dear Lord, thank you for giving me words to live by. Thank you that I can cast all my worries on you. I give you praise for the strength you give me to get through rough times. Often times, I forfeit peace that I could have because I worry. Help me as I learn to cast my cares on you. I need also to remember once I give them to you that they are yours and I shouldn't take them back. Thank you for your love for me. Amen.

Couldn't You Stay Awake?

Ephesians 6:18

"Then he returned and found the disciples asleep. He said to Peter, 'Simon, are you asleep? Couldn't you watch with me even one hour? Keep watch and pray, so that you will not give in to temptation. For the spirit is willing, but the body is weak.'"

Mark 14:37-38

I was reading my Bible one week, and I came upon this passage. I know I have read this many times. On Palm Sunday, during Maundy Thursday services, and various other times I have heard pastors read this same scripture and preach on it. You know how something just clicks in your mind when you read something, and God gives you new insight? That's the way it was for me that day. Let me share what God opened my eyes to.

In this scripture, this is the time when Jesus was praying in the garden of Gethsemane. He had taken some of His followers with Him. He left them to pray while He walked a little farther and prayed diligently Himself. Now for some reason (we don't know why), He went back to check on His followers. He found them asleep. I think He was a little surprised to see them sleeping. He wondered why they couldn't stay awake and pray. They were supposed to be praying for strength against temptation. I am not sure what kind of temptation Jesus was talking about at that time. Jesus went on to say He knew that their spirit was right, but their bodies were weak.

As I was reflecting on this passage a light bulb came on. This scripture is relevant for each of us today. I looked at my own life. The times I am tempted the most are not when I am in prayer. It's not when I am sitting in church listening to the message. It's not even when I am sharing with other Christians about my faith. When I have allowed myself to relax and have "fallen asleep" in my prayer time, I find myself tempted. I can go along and pray diligently, then all of a sudden I find myself busy and my prayer times are not on the top of my priority list. I find I am running circles around myself and I let my Bible and devotion time go by the wayside, thinking I will get to it later. It always amazes me that "later" never comes. I always find something else that needs to be done first. That is Satan's attempt to keep us from studying God's Word. You know yourself from experience that if we miss one Sunday at church, it becomes easier and easier to miss more often. It is during those times Satan comes to us and tries to persuade us that missing church once in a while is okay. He might try to make us think that if we miss praying, God won't miss us because so many other people are praying He won't notice.

So, we become lax or start to spiritually fall asleep. Before long, Satan comes along and tempts us with all kinds of things. Instead of reading the Bible, we pick up a book that is strictly for entertainment purposes, we turn on the TV, or surf the Internet. When a friend invites us to a Bible study, we find all kinds of excuses for not joining. Some of the excuses I have heard and used are, "Well, I can't commit; I am into too many other things," or, "I just don't have the time right now." Another one is, "I'd love to if it was during a different time; that's just not a good time for me." Before long, we wake up from our sleep and wonder what is wrong with our faith. We wonder why we are being tempted so much. Why doesn't Satan just leave us alone?

There is so much around us that is not good for our spirits. As we found out, you can't even watch the Super Bowl without watching

COULDN'T YOU STAY AWAKE?

Satan tempting people with the sexual desires of this world. You go to the movies and hear language that is not proper, or you see scenes in the movies you'd rather not watch. You turn on the TV and some of the ads for products are nothing more than Satan's attempts to tempt us. You drive in your car and see road rage. Every aspect of our lives these days are full of Satan's attempts to get us off track and stray. It's his desire to keep us from becoming the people God wants us to be. We are no longer a Christian nation. Because we aren't, there is temptation everywhere we look and everywhere we go and in whatever we do.

So, what is the answer? We must pray diligently, night and day. We must never fall asleep and allow Satan the opportunity to tempt us. We must pray for strength from God to fight Satan every minute of every day.

The last part of this scripture says the spirit wants to do what is right, but our bodies are weak. We cannot allow our worldly desires to overtake our spirits. We cannot allow our worldly desires to dictate what we want to do. We must allow God's spirit to dwell in us. We must constantly be in a spirit of prayer, renewal, and living out our Christian principles on a daily basis. In the Luke version of this story, it says Jesus prayed so hard that His sweat was like drops of blood falling to the ground. In order to avoid Satan's attempts at us failing and becoming his followers, we must stay awake and pray for strength to fight the battle. We must pray hard! We must stay awake and not allow Jesus to find us sleeping.

Are you sleeping? Are you praying? Where are you in your Christian walk? Don't be like the disciples and fall asleep. Stay awake and pray for strength to fight temptation

> "Always be joyful. Never stop praying. Be thankful in all circumstances, for this is God's will for you who belong to Christ Jesus."
>
> I Thessalonians 5:16-18

L.T. FROG

Prayer: Dear God, I know I need to be in prayer at all times, but it isn't always easy. When I do pray, my mind is often thinking about other things. I can't stay focused. I must be alert at all times if I want to overcome temptation. Put the desire in my heart and give me the spirit to pray at all times. Thank you for the prayer you taught your disciples: "Our Father which art in heaven, Hallowed be thy name. Thy kingdom come, Thy will be done in earth, as it is in heaven. Give us this day our daily bread. And forgive us our debts, as we forgive our debtors. And lead us not into temptation, but deliver us from evil: For thine is the kingdom, and the power, and the glory, for ever. Amen" (Matthew 6:9-13, KJV).

The Passion of the Christ

Matthew 6:14-15, Matthew 18:22

"Jesus said, 'Father, forgive them, for they don't know what they are doing. . . .'"

Luke 23:34

Well, I did it. I went to see the movie. You know the one I am talking about, the movie everyone was talking about a few years ago, *The Passion of the Christ*. After the movie, like so many others, I felt so unworthy of His love. I felt so unworthy of what He had to go through to save me and to allow me to have eternal life. I have done nothing to deserve the gift of what He went through, nor will I ever be able to do enough. Can I love enough? Probably not! What I want to share is some thoughts I had the morning after I had seen the movie. As I was getting ready for church, I was reliving the movie. As I flashed back to the scenes I had watched the night before, some things stuck out in my mind.

If you read the story of Christ's arrest, trial, and crucifixion you will notice several things. One of the first things you might notice is that Jesus was betrayed by a very good friend. At His arrest, He was treated like a criminal. The Jewish leaders had swords and clubs with them. Another thing that happened earlier on was one of His faithful denies even knowing Him. The guards were making fun of Him and beating Him. They talked cruelly to Him. He had to stand and listen as people yell, "...*Crucify Him! Crucify Him!*" (Matthew 27:23). As time goes on, He was forced to wear a thorny crown and was beaten so the thorns tore into His flesh and blood poured out, running down His face. He was beaten, tortured, and then beaten some more. He was forced to carry His own cross. When He fell carrying the cross, He was kicked and made to pick His own cross up and carry it farther. He did all this, all the while being laughed at, mocked, and even spat upon. If you have seen the movie you know the scenes from the Bible I am describing. You get a sense of some of this from Scripture, but portrayed on the screen, it comes alive for you.

I cannot begin to describe the torture and the torment Jesus went through. Can you imagine being given vinegar when you are thirsty? That is what Jesus was given. That morning before church, all those scenes came back to me. Seeing Him on the cross and even being hanged with common criminals—even with one who was laughing at Him. Then, suddenly, with passion in His eyes, "Jesus said, 'Father, forgive them, for they don't know what they are doing.'" (Luke 23:34). Whoa! Wait a minute! He wants His Father to forgive them for what they did to Him? He even said it with passion. Passion described in the dictionary is "the object of any strong desire." So, this wasn't to be a casual thing—He strongly desired for these people to be forgiven.

Now, I have never been spat on, I have never been beaten, and I have never had to wear a thorny crown. I have been lied to, I have been treated improperly, and I have been laughed at. There have been times I have been so mad at those who mistreated me, or my family that I would like to have treated them the same way I was treated. All of these and many more instances surfaced as I replayed the movie over again in my mind, and you know what thought came to me? After watching what Jesus went through for me (me, a person who did not deserve what He did for me), and hearing Him ask for

THE PASSION OF THE CHRIST

forgiveness with passion for those who had done him wrong, how could I not forgive those who have done wrong to me? Who am I to think it is okay to hold grudges, not to forgive, and to hate my fellowmen for the things they have done to me? I have not lived through anything Jesus went through, and He forgave. Who am I not to forgive?

There is another thing that didn't come out in the movie, but knowing Christ as well as I do, I know this to be a fact. Not only did Jesus forgive them, He forgot what they did to Him. He wiped the slate clean. So, as Christians we are not only to forgive others for the way they treat us, we are also to forget the act itself. How many of us have forgiven, but not forgotten? How many of us hang on to the memory of something somebody did to us?

Jesus was treated badly over a few days; it wasn't just a one-time deal. Over the span of our lifetimes, we will be mistreated many times, but what does God say? He says we must forgive more than seven times. We must forgive even if we are wronged seventy times seven. Every time someone does something wrong we are to forgive, even if it's the same person over and over again. Forgive and forget. Move on, don't hold on.

That is some pretty powerful stuff. It won't be easy for some of us to forgive, let alone forget. I don't think it was easy for Jesus, but He did it. The great thing about it is Jesus is on our side, and if we ask, He will help us forgive and forget. We don't have to do it alone. He will be right there helping us, showing us how, and then helping us to erase those memories. Nothing worthwhile is ever easy.

Why do I need to forgive, you may ask? One simple answer is what Jesus says, *"But if you don't forgive others, your Father in Heaven will not forgive your sins"* (Matthew 6:14-15). If you don't want to spend eternity in Heaven and you enjoy fire, then you don't need to forgive; but if you are like me and you want eternal life, and you want to see God and live with peace and joy throughout eternity, then you must forgive and forget.

No one can make that choice for you. It's yours alone. But just remember, since Jesus went through all He went through for us, how can we not forgive others and forget all they have done to us?

The next time we celebrate Christ's resurrection, my prayer is that each reader knows God's love and forgiveness; that this Easter, if you don't know Him, you will reach out to Him and experience the Passion of Christ as He looks to you. I hope you can hear Him as He says, "Father, forgive this person. I have."

"Jesus said, 'Father, forgive them, for they don't know what they are doing.' And the soldiers gambled for his clothes by throwing dice."

Luke 23:34

Prayer: Dear Father in Heaven, you have told me I need to forgive those who hurt me or hurt my loved ones. That's not something I want to do. I am human. When someone hurts me, the first thing I want to do is strike back. I know I must follow your example and forgive. Teach me to do that in my everyday life. Not only did you forgive, but you forgot. Once I forgive, I don't always forget. When the next argument comes, I bring what happened before up once more. Remove those things from my mind that must be forgotten. Help me to wipe my slate clean of any wrong doing others have done to me. Thank you for sending your Son to die on the cross for my sins. Thank you that while you were on the cross your eyes were on me. Thank you for your grace, mercy, and love. Amen.

Winter Storm Watch

Hebrews 11:6 ─────────────────

As I sat in my home in Indiana one February day a few years ago, it was snowing. We had a lot of ice that year and some snow. As I sat and listened to the radio, I heard we had another storm warning out. We were to get snow and then ice and then freezing rain. As I sat and reflected on the winters of past, one thing came to mind. Have you noticed that when the weather people predict a winter storm is coming, the first thing most people do is run out and stock up on the things they think are necessities? It is amazing that when decent weather is around, no one is concerned about getting to the store and stocking up. They go to the store and get what they need, but they don't stock up. Several years ago, when everyone was concerned about the year 2000 coming, the newscasters were telling everyone it would be advisable to go out and stock up on certain items. There were many people who went out and spent money on generators, bottles of water, and all kinds of groceries; all because they feared what "might" happen.

This got me to thinking about faith. There are some people who are no different than the storm stockers. There are two kinds of people. The first kind of people are the ones you rarely see in church. Maybe they only come at Easter and Christmas; and if mom is still around, you might see them on Mother's Day. Other than those times, you rarely see them. Yet many of these same people are "faith stockers." What are faith stockers? These are people who, when faced with trials and tribulation, call everyone they know who will pray for them, get back into church, and maybe even go as far as reading the Bible. They stock up on faith. Then, as the crisis pass, they begin to slip into their old habits. They depend on the faith they have stocked up on to get them through everyday life. I actually know of a man who had heart surgery and life was not looking too good for him. The pastor went to see him in the hospital. During the visit he told the pastor he knew he had slid backwards and he needed to get into church and start trusting God again. After he was home for several weeks, he and his wife attended church faithfully. After a few months he got back into his old habits again. We haven't seen him for some time now.

Some of these faith stockers don't even stock up on their own faith; they rely on their parents' faith stockpile to get them through. I know a family who came to church faithfully while their mom was still alive. They rarely missed a Sunday. Mom died and they attended a few Sundays. After awhile they stopped coming. When someone asked them about coming to church, they got offended and made a comment that their mom had enough faith to get them through life.

The other kind of people are those who don't stock, and they have to run to the grocery store every day or every week. They just get enough to get them by until their next return visit. They don't see the need to stock. They can get by with what they have. They do this because they know it will be just enough to hold them over until they get back to the store. What happens to these people if a storm hits with no warning? They are left unprotected with no stock on hand and maybe not enough to get them by.

So what is the ideal solution? The ideal solution is to be both. That is what I am and many of my friends are. We have stocked up on our faith. We have spent years gathering scripture to fall back on, and we have had years of experience in prayers, so we aren't unfamiliar with how to pray or when to pray; and we have learned over the years to rely on God. We use what we have in stock every day. We use those items on a daily basis. The one thing we don't do is stop stocking our faith. We spend each day replenishing our stock. Now, there are some who replenish weekly. But, that isn't the answer either. They come to church on Sunday mornings and spend an hour in church and maybe an hour in Sunday school, and believe that will get them through to next week. They don't find it necessary to open their Bibles, or pray, or come to an extra service; they have enough to get them by. But what happens if you can't make it to the next week's service? What if you get sick and can't replenish your supply? You can't go to your stockpile because you haven't stocked up. It's been so long since you opened the Bible, you don't know where to start. Prayer, that's foreign to you. You haven't prayed a prayer for a long time. Would you remember the "right" words? What about your trust in God? How is it holding up?

For many of us, we use these items on a daily basis. We never allow our stockpile to deplete. It may get low sometimes, but it is never depleted. We read the Bible on a daily basis; we pray every chance we get. We enjoy being in church, and we find a Bible study or an extra worship service in the week to attend to replenish what we've used since Sunday. When a big storm hits, we aren't worried about it. We have stored up our faith and we have what we use on a daily basis to get us through. There are times when it is necessary to borrow from our family's faith stockpile to help us get through (for instance, prayer, help in finding the right scripture, or sharing with one another). But that is okay, too, because they have plenty to share. Just as neighbors share their stockpiles with others; it is good for Christians to share their faith with others, also. If we replenish our faith every day, then we have plenty to share with others.

So, back to the storm: Which group do you belong to? When storms hit, are you prepared? Or are you a faith stocker, one who stocks up on faith just when the storm hits? Are you a weekly-run-to-the-store-just-to-get-enough-to-get-by person? Or are you one who has stocked up on your faith *and* you replenish that stockpile every day? Are you the kind who has plenty, and whenever the storm hits, you are always willing to share with others; or do you hoard your pile because you don't have enough to share?

The storm is coming. Are you ready?

"And it is impossible to please God without faith. Anyone who wants to come to him must believe that God exists and that he rewards those who sincerely seek him."

Hebrews 11:6

Prayer: Dear God, I know I need to seek you daily through Word and prayer. In this world, there will be trials, disappointments, and temptations. It is only through strong faith in you that I can make it through. Help me as I seek you every day. Put into my heart each day the willingness to search for you. I thank you that as I call out to you, you will answer and be there for me. Amen.

A Frustrating Stain; It Just Won't Go Away

Psalm 55:22

The other day I was doing some laundry. I noticed a stain on one of my shirts. I went to get the stain remover and sprayed some on it. Now, what you are supposed to do is let the stain remover set for a few minutes and then wash the item. Not me! Being the impatient person I am, I decided to spray the remover on it and then proceeded to scrub and work and work to get the stain out. Of course, it didn't work right away, so I had some other removers I used on it. I was getting frustrated because the stain wouldn't come out right away. Finally, after using every remover I had, I decided to use the original stain remover again, let it set, go to bed and forget about it. Guess what happened the next morning? When I got up I had forgotten all about it. I had left the shirt in the kitchen sink all night with the stain remover on it. As I went to the sink to make my cup of tea for the morning, I saw the shirt and the stain had been removed. I thought to myself, if I had only sprayed the remover on it and left it alone instead of working so hard to get rid of it myself, it would have come out a lot easier, and I wouldn't have gotten so frustrated.

As I was thinking about this incident, it reminded me of my own life. How many times have I had a problem in my life and worked and worked and tried to find a solution on my own, but to no avail?

Instead of turning the problem over and letting God handle it, I try to find a solution myself. I want the problem to go away as quickly as it comes, but that doesn't happen. I try many different ways to get the problem to go away; but it's not until I get frustrated and give up and let God handle the problem in His way and in His time, that it goes away.

I also have been working on getting rid of some little bad habits I have. I have tried this solution and that solution, but a lot of times, those bad habits just keep creeping back in. So, what do I do? I try something different. I keep trying until I get frustrated and think I will have this habit forever. Fortunately for us Christians, it doesn't have to be this way. God has told us to give Him our burdens, our worries, and our stains. Psalm 55:22 says, *"Give your burdens to the Lord, and he will take care of you. He will not permit the godly to slip and fall."* All we need to do is go to Him when our problem is bigger than we can handle and give it to Him.

I read somewhere about nailing our problems to the cross. It suggested that when problems creep up, we take those problems and mentally picture ourselves nailing them to the cross and giving them to Jesus. Once we begin thinking about the problems, we look to the cross and see that we have nailed them on it and given them to Jesus. Then we no longer have to fret about them. We may need to nail problems to the cross every day. God doesn't care how many times we nail things to the cross. What He does mind, is us nailing our problems to the cross, coming back and taking them down, and then nailing them back up again. Once we have nailed our situations to the cross, we must never remove them and take them back again. That is like saying to God, "Well, God, I trust you, and I know that you will help me with this problem." When we go get them back, we are saying to God, "Well, I think you can handle it, but I think I could do it faster or better so I am going to try to take care of it myself. I don't need your help, but thanks anyway." Once we give them to God and nail them to the cross, it is important to never take them back again. We must trust God to handle things His way in His own time.

A FRUSTRATING STAIN; IT JUST WON'T GO AWAY

I have learned to nail the needs of my children and their families to the cross and no longer worry about them. Instead, I enjoy my family and let God deal with them. Now I have peace about my family. When I begin to fret, I just stop and think about the day I nailed their welfare to the cross. Then I am at peace knowing God is at work in their lives. One habit I have gotten into every morning when my husband comes and kisses me goodbye as he goes off to work, is to say a prayer for him and my sons-in-law. I pray for safety as they drive to and from work. I do that for my daughters as they travel throughout the day.

I Peter 5:7 reads, *"Give all your worries and cares to God, for he cares about you."* He cares and loves us so much that He wants to handle all the things we are going through. We no longer have to work and work to find a solution. Before we get frustrated and spend all our time in fruitless endeavors trying to get rid of problems, we need to just hand them over to God and know that they will be gone if we are just patient with Him.

I am thinking of having my husband build me a small cross for the bedroom. Then what I want to do is start writing on a piece of paper all the things I want God to handle. The next step for me is to take those pieces of paper and nail them to the cross. When I begin to fret over those things, I want to go in and make a mental note that I have nailed them to the cross and no longer need to worry; God is in charge. I have started doing this mentally and the peace that I have experienced the last few weeks has been tremendous. I can imagine it will only get better.

How about you? Are there some things you need to nail to the cross? Are you working and working on a solution, but finding the problem is not gone? Are you getting frustrated because you've spent so much time on it and it seems to be growing bigger? How about nailing it to the cross and giving it once and for all to God? Then enjoy the peace that God has waiting for you. It's yours for the asking—all you have to do is give it to Him. Are you ready?

"Purify me from my sins, and I will be clean; wash me, and I will be whiter than snow."

Psalm 51:7

"Create in me a clean heart, O God. Renew a loyal spirit within me."

Psalm 51:10

Prayer: Dear God in Heaven, I have at one time or another had to deal with a stain in my life. Stains aren't always easy to get rid of. I scrub and scrub, but I can't do it on my own. It is only when I give those stains to you that I find they are gone. I ask for your help in dealing with those stains. It may be a bad habit, it may be a trial or temptation—whatever it is, help me to nail them to the cross and leave them there. Thank you for allowing me to cast all my cares on you. I give you all the praise and glory for what you are doing in my life. Amen.

Making Disciples

Matthew 28:18

One particular April had been a very rewarding month for me. I was given three opportunities to share God's love and message with people God had put in my path.

The first opportunity came early in April. A friend of mine called and asked me to come to her church and give a talk on prayer. Well, the first thing I did was pray about it. Of course, God urged me to go and do this talk. I could relate to Moses. Just as Moses did not want to go to Pharaoh, I did not want to go do this. Then again, I didn't want to be a Jonah and live in a fish either. I also know that if you don't do God's will, you will not know peace. You don't receive peace until you do what God wants you to do. So I agreed to it. As time came closer I wasn't sure what I was to speak about. My friend did not give me any guidelines. I sat down at the computer to put some notes together, and God took it from there. My talk just fell into place. It's one thing to lead a Bible study and give a devotion to a few friends on Wednesday night; but it is something entirely different to go before women you don't know, to a church you have never been, and speak. I knew from experience that God will never let you go where He won't go with you. I knew God would be there with me. I also had read many times of the strength God gives to His people when He asks them to do what they think is impossible. This was going to be impossible for me if He didn't go with me and didn't give me strength. That was my prayer after He gave me the message; that He go before me and prepare the hearts of the women. I also wanted victory, not for myself, but for Him. I wanted Him to work through me to help others in whatever way He wanted.

I had asked a close friend to go with me and drive. I also wanted a friendly, familiar face in the crowd. When I got there, I was amazed at the age of these women. I thought God had a weird sense of humor. These ladies were several years older than I was. What could I possibly say that they didn't already know? My message (or so I thought) was for the younger, inexperienced women. I gave my message as God directed, thinking I was just practicing and not really teaching these ladies anything. Well, God knows far more than we will ever know. Afterward, I had a couple of ladies come up to me and express that they received something from my message, and I had really helped with their prayer time. Wow! What an awesome God. He knew what these two ladies needed and He provided for them. I left that day feeling a bit humbled that God took me, someone who is not a speaker, whose knees shook the whole times and used me to help someone who needed help! God got His victory, and once again I know "I can do all things through Christ who strengthens me"! I also know where He sends me, He will be, and not only that—He also goes ahead of me to prepare His people to hear His message. All I can say is wow!

The next opportunity to share came just a few weekends later. I was privileged to once again sponsor a friend on her Walk to Emmaus. It is a long and very rewarding weekend for both pilgrim and sponsor. Not only does the pilgrim give up seventy-two hours of her life, but the sponsor gives up a weekend for her pilgrim. There are people who can't understand why I would want to give up my weekend and devote myself to this kind of commitment. The reason is found in the Matthew passage, *"Therefore, go and make disciples of all the nations. . ."* (28:19). I wanted my pilgrim to experience not only God's love, but also I wanted her to have a life-changing experience and grow closer to God. That way, when she comes back to the "real" world, she will teach others, share with others her faith, and encourage those in her circle to become followers of Christ. That is what Christianity is all about. God's desire for us is to share, teach, make disciples, and love one another. Personally, I feel we will all be held accountable for not sharing God's message with others. When I get to Heaven, I know God will point out some of the things I have failed to do as a disciple (just because I am not perfect, nor ever will be until I enter Heaven), but my plan is that God won't say I didn't share His message with others. I may be the only preacher or the only Bible someone may hear or read. As the saying goes, "I am only one, but I am one. I cannot do everything, but I can do something. And what I can do, I ought to do, and with the help of God, I will do." Share your message today; help make disciples for Christ in your neighborhood with your circle of friends and family.

The next opportunity I had that month was on a Friday. One of our church members died. It was one of the ladies I had always looked up to and even wanted to be like. You all have that special someone you admire and want to be like. For me it was Margaret. As the church secretary, I was called and asked if the church could put together a funeral dinner for her family. It would include fifty people. I told the caller I would do what I could and call him back. First, I panicked. I knew some of the ladies who had always done this weren't in the position of doing it now. Their health wouldn't let them. I called a friend who I thought might be able to pull it together, and she wasn't home. I don't think she was supposed to be home. After finding that she wasn't there, God calmed me down and, together with His help, I reached a couple of people who were available to help me. The next thing I knew, within a few short hours, we had more volunteers and food than what we probably needed. I was so happy with the responses I got. God would give me a name, and I'd call and get a response.

We did this out of love for Margaret. I did this out of love and for another reason. Margaret was one of those people I looked upon as a "saint." You all have someone in your church you might consider a saint. I thought if there was anyone who I wanted to be like, it would be Margaret. She showed love to everyone, she shared her faith with me many times, and the smile she had came only from knowing God's love and peace. What a beautiful woman; she was not only beautiful on the outside, but she was a beautiful woman on the inside. You could see God in every aspect of Margaret's life. This was one last thing I could do for her. Margaret gave so much; and it was time we gave back to her, out of love for her and out of love for Christ.

I tell you about these events not to get praise or glory; all that goes to Jesus Christ. I tell you because I know if God can use me, He can use you. I don't have any special talent or abilities. All I have is a willingness to give myself to Him. That is all you have to do—just be willing to give yourself, your time, and your love. You have to move from willingness to trust. You have to trust that God will provide you with all that is needed to do the job He has given you. You have to trust that He will give you strength, and courage; and that He will prepare the way for you. Not only will He prepare the way for you, He will go with you. Once you are willing and trusting, God's peace will surround you and lift you up. It's the kind of peace that only God can give.

Are you willing to teach others, share your faith, and make disciples for Christ? If you don't, who will? Christ is counting on you. Don't let Him down!

> "The Lord replied, 'I will personally go with you, Moses, and I will give you rest—everything will be fine for you.'"
>
> Exodus 33:14

> "The Lord gives his people strength. The Lord blesses them with peace."
>
> Psalm 29:11

Prayer: Dear Father, I don't always like to do the things you call me to do. It is hard, and I don't always have a willing heart. Many times, once I have done those things you've called me to do, I receive more blessings than I give. I want to live in peace, but I can only live in peace if I am willing to do your will. Help me to be open to your calling, knowing you will be with me wherever you send me. Not only will you be with me, but you will also give me the strength I need to do your will. Thank you for the opportunities to share your love and your story with others. Amen.

Jesus Calms the Storm

Matthew 8:23-27, Psalm 27:1-3

Each year, we are faced with the start of a new one. For some, a new year can bring new beginnings; a time to start fresh, and for some, a time of reflection. For some people, old habits and traditions will follow them into the new year. There will be some who will fear the new year's entry into their lives. They have lived and survived the old year. They fear what the new year will bring. Can they survive another year of uncertainty? Can they manage to get through a year of unknowns? On New Year's Eve everyone always wonders what the next year will bring. No one knows the answer to that question. But for those who have fears going into the new year, God clearly gives us some direction.

Psalm 27:1-3 tells us (if we believe):

"The Lord is my light and my salvation—so why should I be afraid? The Lord is my fortress, protecting me from danger, so why should I tremble? When evil people come to devour me, when my enemies and foes attack me, they will stumble and fall. Though a mighty army surrounds me, my heart will not be afraid. Even if I am attacked, I will remain confident."

Wow! Pretty powerful stuff, huh? If we each would remember this verse and take it into the new year, then we would have nothing to fear. If we truly believe the Bible and truly believe God's Word is the truth, then what is there to fear? We say we believe and we know we believe, but what causes the unbelief? The devil tempts us into unbelief.

He begins by putting negative thoughts and ideas into our heads. When those negative thoughts and ideas are put into our heads, we can turn and tell Satan to back off or we can listen to him and continue going off on the wrong path with him. It is our decision to make. I have done both. There have been times I have told Satan to back off and then there have been times I went with the devil's flow until I woke up and realized it was Satan's thoughts and ideas that were causing me grief. What I do next is get into the Scripture to find words that I can put my trust and faith in once more. I ask God again to control my thoughts and to put new, fresh ideas into my mind. Then, I kick the devil out of my mind. It is one, big, control game. It is up to you, who you allow to control your life: the devil or God.

One of the things I have recently found that helps me keep on track is praise music. I used to have the radio on in my car, listening and singing along. That was okay, but I have found if I listen to praise music, I am better equipped to handle things. I don't listen to the radio much anymore. The neat thing is often during the night when I wake up, or early in the morning, I am singing praise songs to God. It is also an excellent witness tool.

Now, sometime during the year, each of us will go through some kind of storm. Whether it is a health issue, financial, the loss of a loved one, or just everyday kinds of storms, we will go through them. How do we deal with these storms? We can trust God to be with us. We can rely on His power and strength and ride it out knowing He is there with us. We can be like the disciples and lose faith in God. What did God tell the disciples when they woke Him? Jesus answered, ". . .Why are you afraid? Do you still have no faith?" (Mark 4:40). We must put our faith in God, we must not be afraid.

JESUS CALMS THE STORM

If we truly believe in God, then He knows what storms we will be going through and He will be there, never leaving us nor forsaking us. God will calm our fears and not let us drown, but only if we trust Him with all that we are.

When New Year comes, go into it with these scriptures on your heart. Know two things about the new year: that the Lord is your stronghold and there is nothing and no one you should fear; and also, that no matter what storms you face this year, God will go through them with you and you will survive as long as your trust is in Him. When the devil decides it's time to put negative thoughts or ideas in your mind, get these scriptures out and read them, ponder them, and write them on your heart. Know that God is God, and nothing is impossible for Him.

> *"Then Jesus got into the boat and started across the lake with his disciples. Suddenly, a fierce storm struck the lake, with waves breaking into the boat. But Jesus was sleeping. The disciples went and woke him up, shouting, 'Lord, save us! We're going to drown!' Jesus responded, 'Why are you afraid? You have so little faith!' Then he got up and rebuked the wind and waves, and suddenly there was a great calm. The disciples were amazed. 'Who is this man?' they asked. 'Even the winds and waves obey him!'"*
>
> Matthew 8:23-27

Prayer: Dear God, I wonder what my future will bring. I worry about my children, or meeting financial obligations, or health issues. I could list lots of things that keep me from having peace in my life. I wonder what storms I will face at the start of each year. If I would only remember you are with me not only in the good times, but also when storms are raging all around me. Help me to keep the faith during those stormy days. Thank you for calming my fears and giving me strength to face my storms. Amen.

The Disciples

Matthew 4:18-22

What do you think about when you think about the disciples? Have you given the disciples much thought? Do you only think of them when you are studying your Bible or a minister talks about them in his sermon?

Let's stop and spend a few minutes thinking about the twelve men who became some of Jesus' closest friends. Jesus called each of them to become fishers of men. He approached them and called out to them, *"'Come, follow me, and I will show you how to fish for people!'"* (Matthew 4:19). I have found nowhere in the Bible where it says any of them declined. What it does say is they dropped their nets, they dropped what they were doing, and they followed Jesus. None of them knew where they were going or exactly what they would be doing. They never were sure where their next meal would come from. They never had a home or a bed to sleep in at night, or at least not one they could call their own. They lived, ate, slept, and fellowshipped with Jesus. Jesus spent time teaching them. They were His students. How would you like to be taught by Jesus? That would be pretty awesome, wouldn't it? I am sure that as they traveled with Jesus, they experienced every emotion known to mankind. Some of them, at times, probably got homesick. Some probably wondered what in the world made them leave everything behind and follow this man.

What amazes me about the disciples is their willingness to leave everything behind and go. They didn't ask questions, they made no excuses for not going, no goodbyes to their families, they just left. I am not sure what motivated them to go. What I do know is they went. This question often comes up in my mind: Would I do that if Jesus asked me to? Could any of us? Could we leave our comfortable homes, our families, and our jobs if He called us to? I can only imagine what our families would say. "What is he doing? He is leaving behind his family, job, and career to follow around some nut who thinks He is Christ? This Christ says He needs her to help spread the gospel? What is she thinking?" This would make *The Montel Williams Show*, for sure.

The question then is asked, where would we be today if twelve men didn't leave behind everything they knew and follow Christ? How would we know about God's saving grace, His love for us, and how Christ died on the cross for us? These men's lives were changed; they no longer were the same. They saw miracles, they heard parables, they felt loved, and in return they loved back. They gave of themselves. When Christ died, it would have been easy to go back and return to their normal lives, but they couldn't. Christ had so touched their lives; they knew they had to pass that on.

Do we have disciples today? I believe we do. There are many people who leave their homes, their lives, and their jobs to go share God's love with people all around the world. I have met several missionaries in my time. I have heard stories of miracles, not from anything they did, but how God intervened in people's lives. I have seen with my own eyes the love missionaries share with the people they work with. I have also seen the pain in these same missionaries, because there is not enough medicine, or no clean water, or not enough resources to help those needing help. I am sure there are times they get homesick and wonder what they are doing. Yet, they keep on keeping on because they know, like the disciples, they have been called.

THE DISCIPLES

I praise God for those first missionaries. I thank God for those twelve men who gave up everything to follow Him. I am thankful they didn't give up when it would have been much easier to do just that.

When you stop and think about it, when we believe and do what God calls us to do, each of us becomes a disciple of Christ. If we love unconditionally, treat others like we would like to be treated, if we share God's message with others, and if we serve others instead of waiting to be served, then we are messengers and followers of Christ. We each can be missionaries in our own neighborhoods, at work, at the gym, or with our friends as we gather. Is Christ calling you? Are you willing to follow Him? Can He count on you to become a fisher of men?

> *"One day as Jesus was walking along the shore of the Sea of Galilee, he saw Simon and his brother Andrew throwing a net into the water, for they fished for a living. Jesus called out to them, 'Come, follow me, and I will show you how to fish for people!' And they left their nets at once and followed him."*
> Mark 1:16-18

Prayer: Dear God, thank you for the twelve men you chose to be fishers of men. They gave up their lives and followed you. Thank you for those men and women of today who also give up their lives to share the good news with others. I, too, can be a fisher of men if I just choose to follow you. I can bring others to Christ if I have a willing heart to follow you and to love others unconditionally. Put the desire in my heart to be like the disciples and share the good news with those I come in contact with. I give you all the honor, glory, and praise. Amen.

Could You Be a Noah?

Genesis 6:9-9:28

We have all heard the story of Noah and his sons throughout much of our lives. We heard it as children growing up, and we've heard ministers preach about Noah's faith and trust in God. We marvel at Noah and his sons being the only people God recognized as "good enough" to save when the flood approached and erased the rest of mankind. We read the story and hear it so often that I think we tend to forget the impact it can have on our lives.

Let's look at Noah for a few minutes. The first thing we notice is God talking with Noah and telling him He plans to destroy the Earth. Nothing will be left except Noah and his family. Also, the only animals that will survive the floods are the ones Noah will take with him on the ark. Stop and think for a minute. If God came to you and told you He was about to destroy the Earth with a major flood, what would your first response to God be? Would you argue, telling God He's making a big mistake? Would you try to persuade God that your brothers, sisters, mom and dad should be included in that list? Would you try to persuade God to include your best friend? Noah's response, as we are told in the Bible, was one of complete obedience. He did everything God commanded. Noah didn't question God, didn't try to persuade God to change His mind, he just did what he was told to do.

◀ L.T. FROG

How many times are we told to do something for God and we spend hours, days, or even months trying to persuade God we aren't right for the job, or He is mistaken about our ability, or we just tell Him no? Very few times are we like Noah and never question God and just go about doing God's business. Another thing to look at is the actual building of the ark. This thing had to be huge. The ark had to hold Noah, his wife, his sons, their wives, and two of every kind of bird, animal, and crawling thing. This boat, as we know, could not have been built overnight. It was built over a period of time. So, now God has told you He is going to destroy the Earth. You finally come to terms with it. Now God wants you to start building this monster in your front yard where all the neighbors can see it. Surely, the neighbors will send you to the local hospital where they are convinced you will be diagnosed as "losing it." It is one thing to know God's plan, but to help Him carry it out? Your family will be laughed at! You know as you try to persuade people of God's plan for the Earth, that you will be made fun of. You will lose your friends, your job; you will no longer be respected. The neighbors will be trying to get you evicted from your house because, as they drive by, it's a constant reminder of how insane you are. You pray about it and are convinced this is what God wants you to do. So, try as you might, you ignore the neighbors and proceed to build this huge ark.

The next thing you do after you have finished the boat is collect animals of all sorts. The neighbors watch as you load donkeys, monkeys, zebras, dogs, cats, elephants, lions, tigers, and bears (oh my!), goats, cows, pigs, sheep, doves, pigeons, owls, spiders, and all the other big and little creatures. What about food? Where are you going to get food for that many animals and for yourself? The sanitation situation alone is enough to make one gasp for breath. The neighbors on each side of you continue to laugh and make fun; they are beginning to hate you because the smell of all these animals in one place at one time is enough to make them sick. There are picket signs, the government comes and tries to persuade you that you're making a big mistake. They tell you if you continue

COULD YOU BE A NOAH?

with this sideshow, they will have to come back and take matters into their own hands.

So now you have been threatened. You ask God again if you heard Him right. You begin to doubt yourself; you begin to doubt God, as well. Even the family is beginning to doubt you. God commands you to carry on. He encourages you and lets you know what you are doing is right. But you wonder, still.

It begins to rain. It rains the next day. It continues to rain for the next few days. There are a few people who are now beginning to wonder if maybe you knew what you were talking about. At the local carpenter shop, men are talking. They are talking about the rain and you. Some still laugh and still make fun, but some are a little more serious now and begin to question your actions. It's been raining now for some time. There are no signs of it stopping. The neighbors are getting panicky. The waters have taken over the garden and the barn where the animals are kept, it just keeps coming. You sit inside the ark and hear the rain. It doesn't stop; it seems to be going on and on. You and your family realize what has happened. God told you it was going to happen, but in the back of your mind you wondered. Now you know for sure. You are comfortable and very thankful that God had found you favorable in His eyes, even though you think you didn't deserve this honor. Then it happens: people are banging on the side of the ark and on the door. They want in. They make excuses for their remarks and actions; they scream with apologies; they desperately want in. They remind you of things they have done for you; they beg and plead. You pray for answers. Should you let them in? Does God really want these people to perish? You no longer find comfort and peace. You hear the screams day and night. It's beginning to wear on you and your family. You pray God will take away your hearing. You can't stand it any longer. You wake up determined to save some people when you realize there is dead silence. There is no sound except the sound of the animals, the rain and the voices of those you have brought with you. Once again, you know what has happened. You fall to your knees and thank God. You gain new strength. You move on. You are now strong and ready to face what is ahead of you.

Each of us, at some time in our lives, will ask God His will for our lives. We want to know what God's plans are for us. We tell God we are willing to do anything for Him. More than likely, He won't respond the way He did with Noah, but if He did, how would we respond? Are we too worried about what our neighbors might think? Are we too proud to build an ark for God? Are we willing to ignore mankind and listen to God, no matter the cost? Do you now turn your back and ignore God's request, afraid of what is ahead? Each of us needs to reread the story of Noah. Put yourself in Noah's place. Make the story of Noah come alive for you. After reading the story, dwell on it, meditate and decide for yourself if you could be a Noah. God may be asking you to do something (maybe not as intimidating or awesome as building an ark) that requires you to step out in faith, just like Noah. God knew He could count on Noah—can God count on you?

"So Noah did everything as the Lord commanded him."

Genesis 7:5

Prayer: Dear Lord, I want to do everything you command me to do. I don't always do it, and, in fact, most of the time I don't. I come up with excuses, turn, and walk away. Thank you for men like Noah, who listened to you. He focused on you and accomplished the things you asked him to do. He is a good example of how I am to live my life. Help me to be more obedient. When I struggle with obedience remind me to look at Noah. I ask for direction for my life as I strive to do your will. Amen.

Dust, Dirt, and Grime

2 Timothy 3:16-17

It is time for confession. Don't you hate those times when you know you have to confess and don't want to? Well, that time has come. Most of you ladies will laugh and some of you will be nodding your head yes, knowing you are guilty, too. Some of you men will be thinking of tasks you hate to do, as well. My confession is simple. I hate doing housework. I don't mind sweeping once in a while, but I hate to dust. I like doing dishes once in awhile but am grateful for the dishwasher in our newer home. I like washing clothes because I can throw them in the washer and run off to do other things. It is the same with the dryer. Now, my house is clutter free. I straighten up my house every day and it looks pretty nice, just don't look at the dust or the cob webs. I would much rather be outside planting flowers, pulling weeds, or even mowing the grass. Anything, as long as it deals with the outdoors.

I realize the importance of cleaning. It is necessary to get rid of dust, grime and dirt. I also know if I don't do it weekly, it can build up. If it builds up, it can take me a whole lot longer to get rid of the dust, dirt, and grime. I have done both. I have cleaned weekly and I've let it go.

Recently when I was cleaning, God shared some more of His

insights with me. That is what weekly church service is all about. It's plain and simple. During the week we accumulate dust, dirt and grime in our own lives; when we worship on Sunday morning that is the time to rid ourselves of those things. We come to church on Sunday not only to fill our cup, but also to clean our cup. We need a time to clean our cup before we can fill our cup and get ready for the next week. There are times I just want to come to church to be filled. I don't want to clean. I don't want to take the time to scrub off those dusty marks, or dirty cracks or clean the grime left behind by something or someone in my life. But you know what? It's just like home. If I don't clean weekly, it builds and builds. The next thing I know, I have to spend hours cleaning my life and not being able to enjoy the good times.

There are some tasks at home you do daily—making the bed, for instance, or doing the dishes, or picking up the newspapers. They are just little things to help your home look nice on a daily basis. That is where Bible study and prayer come in each day. I have found if I read my Bible and pray every day, I don't have to scrub as hard on Sunday mornings. I go to Wednesday night Bible study and that really helps with the dust, and grime during the week. Just like with the house, though, I have to be diligent and do these things on a daily basis. If not, it takes extra work on Sundays.

My mom always taught me you had to do Spring House Cleaning and Fall House Cleaning—those certain things you don't do but once or twice a year. After we would do them, how the house would shine. I do attempt to do the spring and fall cleaning, not only in my home, but also in my life. I think it is important for each of us to stop and reflect on what areas in our lives need extra cleaning. What are those things in our lives we really do need to discard? What areas need to be scrubbed a little more than usual? I enjoy going on women's retreats. I use those times to really clean, scrub, and polish. Just like the home after a good cleaning, my life shows the work I've had done, and I am ready to move on until the next time.

How are the dust, dirt, and grime in your life? Do you go to church each Sunday just to be filled up, or do you take the time to

DUST, DIRT, AND GRIME

clean yourself as well? Do you do the necessary tasks each day so you won't have to clean so hard? Wednesday night is a wonderful time to set aside to do a little extra cleaning each week. And what about the spring and fall cleaning? When is the last time you have done those tasks?

My prayer is that you take time each day through prayer and Bible study to clean; and on Sundays you go to clean your cup, as well as fill it. God will show you those areas that need a good spring and fall cleaning.

"Create in me a clean heart, O God. Renew a loyal spirit within me."

Psalm 51:10

"People who conceal their sins will not prosper, but if they confess and turn from them, they will receive mercy."

Proverbs 28:13

Prayer: Dear Father, you know all too well my faults; you know I don't like to clean. There are times in my life that I need a good scrubbing and cleaning. I need to rid myself of those things that hide the beauty of my life. I need to clean myself from hurt and pain caused by something I did or something someone else did. Thank you that I can come to you and be cleansed. Give me the courage to clean my life; and help me to be diligent every day to study your Word and grow closer to you. I ask all these things in thy name. Amen.

God Gave You a Talent: Are You Hiding It?

Matthew 25:14-30

I once wanted to know the difference between gifts and talents, so I looked both words up in the dictionary. There are several meanings for each word. The definition I decided to use for gift was from *Merriam-Webster:* "something voluntarily transferred by one person to another without compensation." Next, I went to talent and found this definition: "a marked, natural ability that needs to be developed; a special, often athletic, creative, or artistic aptitude."

I found this to be quite interesting. Let's look at gifts for a second. In plain English, it means someone giving something to someone else without pay. I give you a sweater just because I want to. I don't expect anything in return. I give out of love for you. Now let's look at talents. In plain English again, it means I have a talent. I can do something well and with a little help and some development, I can be creative.

Now here is my take on the two words: God gives us a gift when we are born. Not only does He give us the gift of life, but I also think in each of us, he gives us the gift of a talent. He gives it to us out of His love for each of us. He loves us so much that he wants to shower gifts on us. I think at some point in our lives we find "our" talent. It is up to us how we use or develop that talent. It may take years and some real soul-searching to discover it. I think it can even take someone else to tell us about a talent we have not discovered yet. It can even take one circumstance in our lives to find the talent God has given us. But I am convinced now more than ever that God gives us each a talent.

As a child, I was not musically inclined. I did not have the ability to be a cheerleader (even though I tried out year after year and got turned down), I was not artistic, and I certainly was not an orator. So I went through my teenage years thinking God did not give me any kind of gift when it came to talents. I was given the gift of life, wonderful parents and family, but that was about it. It wasn't until I was in my 40s that I discovered my talent; it first hit me when I was in college. I had to write a paper in some English or journaling class. I don't even know what happened to the paper. But I remember that I wrote about a softball game and the parents watching the game. I can't remember exactly what it was all about. The thing that hit me was, after we had turned it in, a few days later the professor decided to read a few of these. I knew I had no talent, so I didn't think anything about it. She read a few and they were good. Then she made a comment that she had saved the best for the last. She said to pay close attention, because you could feel the excitement and you would be able to feel as if you were there for all the action. As she began to read, I realized it was my paper. I even began to get excited as she read, and I felt I was in the middle of the action I had written about. After class, she commented on how well I did on the paper. Some of the other students even mentioned it to me. I began to wonder, "Did God give me the gift of writing?" A few years went by and before I knew it, I was writing devotionals on a full-time basis. Not only was I writing them, but people from all over were asking me to send my articles to them.

Okay, now why did I tell you this story? Well, it's not to tell you how talented I am or how "great" I am. The point of the story is this: God gives each of us a talent. He gives us a talent out of love for us. He really doesn't expect us to repay Him. In fact, there

GOD GAVE YOU A TALENT: ARE YOU HIDING IT?

is no way we could ever repay God for all He has given us. But, if God loves us so much, shouldn't we love Him enough to share with others the talent He has given us? That is why I write. I write not because I think someday I will get paid for the talent that God has given me. I write because 1.) God gave me the talent in the first place, and 2.) I do it out of love for Him.

In Matthew 25:14-30 we read about the man who was going on a journey and called his slaves together. He trusted them with his possessions. He gave each of his slaves what he thought each had the ability to possess. You know the story. Each slave did something different with the talent he was entrusted with. The last slave caught my eye. He did nothing with the talent he had. All he did was hide it until the master came back. The master was not happy about it. So he took the talent away and gave it to the other slaves. This guy had a talent that he did not use. His talent was taken away from him. In my childish mind, I am afraid that if I don't use the talent God has given me to use, it will be taken away from me. I will be talentless. I will have done nothing to help God's kingdom grow. Someday, I may be multitalented but for now, I have a talent that I can't hide. I use it for God's glory, not my own.

We all have talents, including you! I don't care how old, how crippled, or how inadequate you may feel. You have a talent. We may even have the same talent. You may use your talent in a different way than I do. I have a friend who has the same talent of writing I do, but she does hers in poetry form and does it beautifully. You may be multitalented. God bless you if you are. You may not have discovered your talents yet; if you haven't, search for it. Ask your family and friends, seek your pastor's advice, and seek God. God will let you know your talent. Strive not only to find your talent, but also to use it once it's found. What a wonderful world this would be if we all found the talent God gave us and used it for God's glory out of our love for Him.

Read the story in Matthew 24:14-30 and see what happened to the man who hid his talent. Are you hiding God's gift of talent under the ground? Will your talent be given away? My prayer for you is God will reveal your talent and you, out of love for Him, will share it with others.

> *"To those who use well what they are given, even more will be given, and they will have an abundance. But from those who do nothing, even what little they have will be taken away."*
>
> *Matthew 25:29*

Prayer: Dear Lord, you have given me a talent. Show me, Lord, my talents. Put the desire in my heart to use my talents, not for my own glory, but for yours. May the praise I receive from using my talents go to you, for you have given me all things good. Thank you for choosing me to be your instrument to share your message with others. Amen.

Will and Power

Philippians 4:13

I was home visiting my daughter recently. She has often struggled with weight issues. We were once again discussing it. She said, "Mom, I just don't have willpower."

Later, I was thinking about what she said. How many of us have said the same thing about breaking a habit, or losing weight or just trying to accomplish something? We just don't have the willpower to accomplish the task.

I look at the term "willpower" and I see it not as a "term" but as two separate words combined to make one. The first word is "will." A couple of terms in the thesaurus for "will" are "choice" or "preference." So as I look at "will," I think about what choices we are making. Are we choosing to follow our own preferences? Or are we choosing to follow God's will for our lives?

The next word is "power." Again, according to the thesaurus, we see that this word can mean "strength," "force," "energy," and "vigor." When we have power, we can pretty much accomplish anything.

In the past, I decided to follow my own will and do things my own way. Every time I tried to accomplish things, I would get in the middle of something and realize I had no power to finish on my own.

I would lose the energy needed to accomplish the task. Sometimes I would even fail if I tried to accomplish some tasks on my own.

I soon realized that the more I began to follow God's will for my life, the more things I accomplished. I had the power to succeed. I had the energy and the vigor to get the job done. There were times I had amazing strength to get several things done at one time. I even accomplished things I thought I could never do before.

So, what was the difference? I was following God's will in my life. When we follow God's will for our lives and we do the things He wants us to do, He will give us the power, strength, energy, and the vigor to accomplish those things. In Philippians 4:13 it says, *"For I can do everything through Christ, who gives me strength."* If we are living according to God's plan for our lives, then He will give us the strength we need to follow through. In Psalm 29:11 it says, *"The Lord gives his people strength. The Lord blesses them with peace."*

If I am following God's will for my life, I can count on His strength and His power to help me accomplish the things He has set before me. When I became president for our local United Methodist Women's group here in Texas, I knew it was a task I could not handle. I would be in charge of four circles; I would have to answer not only to the church, but also to the UMW Executive Board; I would have to write reports and share with the Conference and District leaders as well. I would be in charge (with help from the board) of putting together a Sunday observance for United Methodist Women. I would be expected to speak before the congregation on UMW Sunday, doing many of the tasks Pastor Mike did every Sunday. I am not a speaker, nor have I ever been a speaker. It would have been easy for me to turn this down and walk away. Yet, after much prayer, I sensed this was God's will for me. At the time I am writing this, I am on my second year. I made it through UMW Sunday, I have gotten my reports done in a timely manner, and I have done things I know I could not have accomplished on my own. It has been through God's power, His strength, and Him giving me the energy I needed to accomplish what He has set before me. As the old saying goes, "If He brings you to it, He will give you the power to get through it." (Okay, maybe I changed it a little.)

WILL AND POWER

I have been asked to lead Bible studies in the past. Once again God's power and energy allowed me to accomplish the task, not because I wanted to lead the Bible studies, but because I was following His will.

For me, it is easy to know the difference. When I am in the middle of doing something and I feel like I am in a maze, I have to ask myself if I am following God's will or if I am doing something I just want to do. If around every corner there is a wall, or if I lose the energy and the excitement, then you can bet I am doing my will and not the Lord's. I also don't have the peace that comes with following God's will, let alone His power. That's when I must politely bow out and excuse myself from whatever I am doing.

We do have to be careful because Satan likes to deceive, and he will come along with a false sense of power. He will allow us to think we can do things on our own without God's help. We may even accomplish things on our own without God's power and strength. Too many times, though, we get a false sense of pride when we do that. We start thinking we are great; we did this without help from anyone. We have to be aware of where our power comes from. Satan is always ready to tear us down and destroy us.

The last thing we need to be reminded of, is to always to be ready to give God the praise He deserves for the power He has given us to accomplish those tasks. I can do nothing without Him. There have been times people have come up and wanted to praise me for the things I have accomplished. My reply has always been and will be, "Don't thank me or give me the praise. Just praise God and thank God that I was willing to be used by Him." I am the instrument and God is the musician. Or, in my case, I am the keyboard and God is the writer.

Are you at a point where you are following God's will? Is God calling you to do something, but you are afraid of failure? Don't be afraid, God's power and strength are yours. If He is bringing you to it, He will give you all the energy, power and strength to accomplish great things for Him!

L.T. FROG

"For I can do everything through Christ, who gives me strength."

Philippians 4:13

Prayer: Dear Lord, it is not always easy to follow your will. I want to be in charge of my own life. I want the power to choose. Many times when I do follow my own way, I lose sight of what my goal is or I lose the will to get things done. It is when I relinquish my will and follow your will for my life that I find power and strength to accomplish the tasks you have given me. Thank you for how you are working in my life. Amen.

More Than a Glass of Water

John 4:10

I had the opportunity recently to view a memorial service for a man named Jake. I knew Jake and his family. Jake had been a minister and had retired. At the memorial service, another pastor was one of the first to speak. He spoke of a time when he was on top of the world. He had a large church, one that was televised on Sundays. If you stayed home from church, that is who you watched. Everything was going his way. Through a set of circumstances he lost his job, his church, friends abandoned him, and church officials were no longer ones he could count on. One day he opened the door and there was Jake. He went on to speak about how Jake stayed with him and was a friend to him when he had lost everything. He spoke very eloquently of Jake. As a final remark, he said that if he had been given the opportunity to witness before God about Jake, there is only one thing he would do that would describe him. He would take a glass of water, hold it up to God and say nothing. Powerful image, isn't it?

When I was watching this, I was in the middle of a bout of influenza and was taking medicine. My mind was a bit fuzzy. All week, I kept thinking about this image. What does holding a glass of water imply? On Saturday, my mind cleared and it hit me. When it did, I thought, "Wow that was powerful!" God speaks to us throughout the Bible, telling us He is the living water. He is the only way to eternal life. If we come to Him and drink His water, we will thirst no more. When this man had lost everything, Jake was there to remind Him God was still there. Everyone else abandoned him in his time of need, but it was Jake that offered God to him. When we have nothing left, we still have God. When there is no hope, we still have hope in God and in eternal life. God will never leave nor forsake us. The second part of Hebrews 13:5 says, "*I will never fail you. I will never abandon you.*" What Jake was doing was offering to walk alongside this man, to be there for him, to remind him that God had not abandoned him. God couldn't physically be there, so he sent Jake. Jake represented God offering this man living water: hope for a better tomorrow, hope in eternal life.

Once again, I thought about myself. Do I offer others living water? Do I offer to walk alongside them when they have no hope left, or do I follow the crowd and abandon people? How do I respond? How would I want others to respond to me? It is one thing to talk about faith, but it is quite another to offer faith to others when their worlds are in turmoil. A glass of water will never mean the same to me. The next time I see a glass of water, I will think of Jake and realize that even in his death, He showed others how to live for God. What a powerful statement about one man's life.

What do you offer people? I hope you can offer them a glass of water. I also hope you are willing to accept that glass of water when it is offered to you. God bless Jake!

> *"Jesus replied, 'If you only knew the gift God has for you and who you are speaking to, you would ask me, and I would give you living water.'"*
>
> *John 4:10*

Prayer: Dear Lord, thank you for sending people into my life who walk beside me and help me through tough times. When I have lost faith in people, thank you for sending people into my life who offer me water. As I take and drink from this water, it once more gives me hope in eternal life. Help me to offer help, comfort, and strength to those around me who need it most. I love you, Lord, and I thank you for the water you have given me. Amen.

Don't Ask Me to Leave

Ruth

"But Ruth replied, 'Don't ask me to leave you and turn back. Wherever you go, I will go; wherever you live, I will live. Your people will be my people, and your God will be my God. Wherever you die, I will die, and there I will be buried. May the Lord punish me severely if I allow anything but death to separate us!'"

Ruth 1:16-17

You will recognize this from the story of Ruth in the Bible. Naomi had two sons, Mahlon and Kilion. The two sons were married to Ruth and Orpah. As the story progresses, Naomi's husband and two sons die, leaving her behind with just the two daughters-in-law. Naomi decides to head back to Judah. On the way, she urges these two young women to leave her and go back to their families. After some discussion, Orpah agrees to leave her, but Ruth is insistent: She wants to stay with Naomi. That is where the above scripture comes into play. This is certainly a love story between two women. The friendship they share is about sacrifice, devotion, and caring for another.

Another story I am reading now portrays the same kind of love and friendship. I am reading the *End of the Spear* by Steve Saint. His father, Nate, was one of five missionaries who were killed by the Waodani tribe when he was young. Instead of trying to seek revenge, Steve stays with his aunt Rachael and lives among the same tribe that killed his father. At some point, he returns to the United States. He marries, has a family, and lives the good life. He is a successful businessman. His children are all in school and are doing really well. When his aunt dies back in Ecuador, he goes to bury her. While there, he meets up with some of the same men who speared his father. The men who killed Nate are a little fearful for their lives, not knowing how Steve will react when he arrives back in Ecuador. He reaches out in love; many of them were his friends growing up. They ask him to come and live with them and to teach them. This would mean giving up a nice business, a good home, giving up all the comforts of life, uprooting his family, and living in the jungle. God calls Steve to do just that, but he isn't sure about his wife and children. To make a long story short, they are all willing to go with Steve and live in the jungles of Ecuador, among some of the same people who believed it was okay to spear someone when they were angry, frightened, or feel threatened.

In both cases, love was demonstrated beyond anything any of us could imagine. This was God's love, the kind of love God is teaching us about in the Bible. Sacrificial love, love that says I can love my enemies, love that is made possible through God.

I loved my mother-in-law. She was a wonderful woman. She was not godly, but she was a kind woman. Could I live with her forever? No, I would not have been able to move in and live with her—we were too different. We did not share the same goals in life, or even the same interests. I loved her very much, but to live with her would be another thing. Yet, this is exactly what Ruth did in the Bible. She ignored her own interests, beliefs, and gave up returning to her own family just to stay with Naomi. She just didn't stay with Naomi, she took care of her. It was noted throughout the community how much Ruth did for Naomi; people could see the love Ruth had for her. Do we have that kind of love today? Are we willing to give up everything we have to take care of someone else? Are we willing to set aside our own needs and desires to take care of someone?

Steve Saint writes in his book about having to wash his clothes in the river, eat monkey meat, walk long distances to get to places, and not having any comfort. He sleeps on the floor; he eats food without asking what it is. There are no hospitals or doctors. He is in the thick of the jungle. Why? Because God has put a love for these people in Steve's heart. These people don't know it isn't okay to spear someone "just because." They have never been taught to forgive and forget. They don't know anything about God's love for them. If Steve doesn't teach them, who will? His wife was reluctant to go at first. She was not sure she could give up the comforts of a home. What draws her is what she sees in Steve's eyes and his heart. She sees the love Steve has for the Waodani tribe.

Look at us today. We have all the comforts anyone could ask for. We have microwaves, refrigerators, stoves, TVs, cell phones, radios, cars—life is good for us. What are we missing? We are missing the kind of love for one another that Steve has found for the Waodani people, or that Ruth had for Naomi. Instead of reaching out to those who are different, we argue about where they are going to live. Instead of reaching out to those who have committed crimes, we lock them up and throw away the key. Sometimes we don't even get along with our own neighbors. We aren't even willing to take the time to cross the street and reach out to our neighbor in love, let alone halfway across the world.

We have children going hungry, food banks that are nearly empty, and people running around naked because we can't sacrifice one can of food or give up one piece of clothing. Yet, we say we are a nation that loves people. We are a nation that loves things. We are a nation that loves our own kind. When disaster strikes, we are right there helping out, doing all we can. We give sacrificially, we give out of love, but after a few months, things go back to normal and we forget what Jesus taught us.

He taught us to love one another. We are to love our neighbors as ourselves. Yes, that may mean making sacrifices, living with a little bit of discomfort, and yes, even reaching out to others who are different. It may mean going across the street and sharing God's love with your neighbor. It may mean reaching out to a child who has nothing. It may mean giving a job to the man who can't speak English, or the woman whose husband has left her to raise their children by herself. Or it may simply mean loving your enemies, even if they hurt and persecute you.

Most of us accept the Bible as being inspired by God. We think of the Bible as God's teachings, His instructions on how to live. If we believe that, we have to believe God wants us to love everyone just as He loves us. He wants us to love just like Ruth, Steve, and many of the other saints in the Bible. We can't pick and choose the parts we like and ignore the parts we don't like.

I am just as guilty as anyone. I think I love everyone, but if God asked me to go eat monkey meat, live in the jungles of Ecuador among those who have speared people in the past, could I? Could I give up my way of life to go and live with someone, knowing I would have to put my own desires and goals in life on hold?

These are all questions we all have to ask ourselves. There may come a time God will ask each of us to step out of our comfort zone and show love toward someone we might be uncomfortable with. What will your reply be? My prayer is that each of us we will be able to respond just like Ruth . . . don't ask me to leave and turn back.

Prayer: Dear Lord, Thank you for missionaries, who give up the comforts of life to help others know the truth about you. Thank you also for the men and women in the Bible who teach me how to live and love others. I know I should follow by example, but it is not always easy. Help me to reach in myself and find the desire to follow you and help others in doing so. Amen.

We Don't Always Feel Like Having an Attitude for Gratitude

Philippians 1:3-4

In the last few years, we have heard a lot of people talking about how in November we need to have an "attitude for gratitude." For the most part, I agree with this statement, but yesterday was one of those days that I would disagree. Instead, I would suggest to you there are days you don't feel like having that kind of attitude. An attitude for gratitude is not something you can experience when you have just been told a friend has been killed in an accident. An attitude for gratitude is not something you can easily have when almost everyone around you is fighting cancer. An attitude for gratitude is not easily available when your world is being turned upside down and life doesn't always seem fair. So what is the answer for *those* days?

Well, my friends, let me share with you. After the shock sat in about my friend's death, pain and a sense of loss began to fill me. I began to go through the grieving process. The day seemed dark and dreary, even though the sun was shining. Memories of conversations we had began to flood my thoughts. We had just spent the previous Saturday evening together at a Sunday school class party. We laughed and had a wonderful time. All the friends in our class commented that we couldn't wait for the Christmas party—it would be full of fun and surprises. After that evening I began feeling like the class had gelled. We had become one in Christ. It was a wonderful feeling. Now, there was a hole.

I went to bed not having an attitude for gratitude. As the new day began, I started having a different attitude about the situation. I was still hurting and mourning my friend, but an attitude for gratitude for my friend began to fill me. Gratitude is defined as "the state of being grateful." As I thought about him and my friends who are fighting cancer, I became very grateful. I am not grateful that he died and they are fighting cancer, but I am grateful for two very important reasons. The first reason is the fact that they are Christians. They know Christ, believe in Christ, and have a personal relationship with Him. They show love and they shower other people with love; this is Christ's love shining through them. The second reason I am grateful is because I have had a relationship with these people. I am a far better person because of things they've said to me or things they have done for me. Because of them, my life has changed.

During a Sunday school class, my friend Scott gave me some food for thought. He asked me to reconsider a decision I had made. He offered some insight into a situation I really hadn't thought about. One of my close lady friends who is dealing with cancer gave me love, and support and encouraged me when I was going through some difficult days in my early days of being UMW president. She lifted me up when I was down. As I think about each friend who is suffering, I realize they all have been there for me. They have encouraged me in some way. They have reached out to me. That allows me to be in an "attitude for gratitude" when I think of them.

It is not always easy to be in an attitude for gratitude. If we allow ourselves time to go through the hurting, the loss, and the disappointment, then later we can begin to have an attitude of thankfulness for what is happening in our lives. As we look back on situations, we can always be thankful God was there, walking alongside us or maybe even carrying us, allowing His strength to get us through tough times. In the days ahead, I will be going to a funeral or a memorial service for my friend. I will mourn his loss. I will once again be reminded how short life is and how we are never promised tomorrow. I will be reminded I don't grieve for him; he has been given his reward and earned his crown. I grieve for myself and my loss, his friendship and love. Then, after a time of mourning, I can return to my attitude for gratitude and be thankful I was in his presence while here on Earth. I can begin to be thankful for the relationship we had and the relationship he had with Christ. Yes, we all need an attitude for gratitude. It will come to each of us in our own time, or better yet, in God's time.

Do you have an attitude for gratitude? Even in death, sickness, and times of distress, if we allow God to be a part of our lives, we can have such an attitude. Remember this Thanksgiving and every day to count your blessings not your losses. God bless.

"And now, just as you accepted Christ Jesus as your Lord, you must continue to follow him. Let your roots grow down into him, and let your lives be built on him. Then your faith will grow strong in the truth you were taught, and you will overflow with thankfulness."

Colossians 2:6-7

Prayer: Dear Lord, there are people who you send into my life to be my friends, my mentor, and to teach me to be a better person. Sometimes these people come and go for whatever reason. When these people leave me, there is a hole. I feel their absence and grieve. Help me to be grateful for the time you have shared them with me. Teach me to look upon these times, not with sadness, but with joy for the time I had with them. Help me also to be the kind of friend, mentor, or teacher to others that they were to me. Bless each one of these that have left me and moved on. Amen.

Childhood Games, Not So Fun!

I Samuel 16:6-8, Psalm 139

Remember those childhood games we used to play? You know, Red Rover, or kick ball, and then there was dodge ball. These were games where kids had to choose others to be on their teams. You might have played different games, but certain kids were always leaders, and the leaders would choose their teammates. I remember those days. Of course, I was always the kid that got picked last. I was not athletic or popular and not very strong. I was a small child. I could never understand why the smart, strong, and often popular kids were always the team captains. It was never the puny, weak, or lonely kids who got to be team captains.

Everybody wanted to be the team captain's buddy. I would always try to play my best so the team captain wouldn't be disappointed in me and maybe I would be picked earlier next time. I wanted to make my teammates proud of me. Well, somehow I always disappointed them and myself. For a long time, I had low self-esteem. I always wanted to be better, or be someone else, or be stronger, or popular, or whatever it would take for people to like me. My brother and sister were older than me. They were popular. My sister had the beauty; my brother had the charm. He started a band and was the lead singer. Needless to say, he had girls all over him and the band.

My sister dressed well. She was the first granddaughter, so she got all the new clothes. I got the hand-me-downs. I used to resent it; now, I don't even give it a second thought. I am okay with not being popular, strong or athletic.

What changed? God showed me how different things are. One of the people in the Bible who God pointed me to was Moses. Moses murdered a man. He was not popular with the Israelites. He ran off to a different life before he was called to serve God. Paul is one of my favorite people. Paul had Christians killed. Yes, he was popular, but with the wrong crowd. God showed him what life was all about. Zacchaeus was a Jewish tax collector. Now, talk about an unpopular man! Then there was the man who was lying on a mat. His friends had to lift him down through the roof of a house so Jesus could heal him. Talk about weak! This man couldn't even walk to Jesus. He had to be carried. Oh, and what about the Samaritan woman who wouldn't even go to the well when the other women did? She went at a different time because she was an outcast. These are people Jesus mentioned in the Bible. They are major Bible characters. Each of these men and women turned their disappointments, heartaches, and weaknesses over to God and became important to our faith today. Each of these characters, in their own stories and circumstances, teach us how to live, love, and become more Christ-like. They were popular but not until they came to Christ to be used by Him and for Him.

Look at the kings. We would consider it an honor to be a king. We could have everything and anything. All we would have to do is mention something and we could have it. Let me name you a few kings that weren't so honorable. Herod was the ruler and king of Galilee. Herod had John the Baptist arrested and killed. The Pharaoh (which is another word for king) of Egypt made slaves out of the Israelites. He was not a kind king. These are just a couple of examples of kings who might have been popular, but they followed the wrong crowd and worshiped the wrong god.

As I began to study the Bible more, and as I began to grow in Christ, I soon realized it is not the popular, the strong, or the Biblical scholar who God always calls to do His work. It is often the ones who are chosen last; those standing last in line are the ones God calls to do His work. The weak often have something to teach the strong. It is through our weakness and our strength in Christ that we become strong and can withstand the challenges of life. Likewise, the unpopular person has something to share with the popular. It is when we don't follow the crowd but follow Christ that we become popular, not with our fellow human beings, but with Christ. I love the saying, "God doesn't call the equipped, He equips the called." He will give us what we need to do the job that He has called us to do.

If I could have known when I was child what I know now, if I could be team captain, I wouldn't call the popular, the strong, or the athletic. I would look through Jesus' eyes and choose those who were willing to humble themselves and become children of God.

God chose who He chose for a reason. God chose you and me for a reason; not because we are popular, or athletic, or strong, He called us because we are willing; willing to step out and be used for Him and by Him. Be proud of who you are. Be thankful for all the Moseses, Pauls, Zacchaeuses, and the shunned women who are willing to be used by God. I choose God's side—which side do you choose? Let us all give praise, thanks, and glory to our Team Captain because He chose us.

> *"You made all the delicate, inner parts of my body and knit me together in my mother's womb. Thank you for making me so wonderfully complex! Your workmanship is marvelous—how well I know it."*
>
> Psalm 139:13-14

Prayer: Dear Lord, thank you for making me who I am. Remind me Lord, that unlike so many of my peers you look inside my heart and see me for who I am; and you love me for who I am. Remind me that I don't have to be popular, or wealthy, or even

L.T. FROG

have beauty, to be called a child of God. When I think I can't be called into service because I don't have what it takes, remind me of Moses, Paul, Zacchaeus, and the woman at the well. Thank you for equipping the called and not calling the equipped and using people the world sees as unfit. May I always be mindful of what team I am on. Amen.

Help in Troubled Times

Psalm 9:9, Psalm 32:7

Psalm 46:1-3 reads:

> "God is our refuge and strength, always ready to help in times of trouble. So we will not fear when earthquakes come and the mountains crumble into the sea. Let the oceans roar and foam. Let the mountains tremble as the waters surge."

Verses 6-7 read:

> "The nations are in chaos, and their kingdoms crumble! God's voice thunders and the Earth melts! The Lord of Heaven's Armies is here among us; the God of Israel is our fortress."

In verse 10 it says, "Be still, and know that I am God! . . ."

If ever there were a time nations were in chaos, it is now. There have been times of trouble in the last year. People have lost jobs, homes, and even money. The news media and government tell us it will be at least another year before things turn around. My son-in-law lost his job, another son-in-law could lose his job, and there is talk of my husband's company going bankrupt. If not bankrupt then a restructuring, in which case my husband would have to take a huge pay cut. People are in turmoil. Job fairs have thousands of people showing up, standing for hours for a handful of jobs. People who once never thought about flipping hamburgers or taking orders, are now competing for those jobs. Men and women who had large sums of cash stashed away now find the money is gone or soon will be; they are hoping the market will turn around so they will once again see green in their accounts. People who have dreamed of owning their own homes now are looking at losing their homes. Those who have lost homes are wondering how soon they will be the next victim. It is not a pretty sight for many people.

I am not panicking. I am not losing sleep. I am okay. When everyone else is in a panic, how can I stay calm? Because I can take comfort in the scriptures I found in the Bible. My husband called me this morning with more bad news about his company. It would have been easy for me to panic, cry out, and lose it. After hanging up the phone, I picked up my morning devotion and guess what scripture I came across? You're right—Psalm 46. I can boldly say God is my refuge and my strength. I have been through some mighty tough times already in my life. I have seen what God has done. I have seen Him pull us through when I was sure we would sink. I know He will be my Helper in these troubled times. I know that when I can't trust the market or the government and I can no longer put my faith in my husband's job, I can put my faith and trust in God. He will be there when no one else will.

What is a fortress? According to the thesaurus, it is a stronghold, a fort, a castle. It goes on to say that a fortress acts as protection; something that is impossible to get through. The scripture says, ". . . the God of Israel is our fortress" (Psalm 46:7). In other words, if I go to God, He will protect me. The enemy will not get to me. Oh, I may still have trouble, but God will be there fighting for me all along. You see, it is not money that makes me happy. It certainly helps, but I can't take it with me. My house is nice to have, but I don't need it to make me happy. Do you think the disciples had homes? They were constantly traveling about. I don't need a mansion, just something to protect me from the elements. I am sure God will provide. It might not be up to my standards, or what I have been used to, but God will provide. Cars, jewelry, furniture—these are just things. They are nice to have, and I would hate to lose them, but still, they are things. They aren't what makes me who I am.

There is another passage found in Philippians 4:11-12 that spoke to me:

"Not that I was ever in need, for I have learned how to be content with whatever I have. I know how to live on almost nothing or with everything. I have learned the secret of living in every situation, whether it is with a full stomach or empty, with plenty or little."

See, I have lived on almost nothing before. I know what it is like to live from paycheck to paycheck, wondering where the next meal is going to come from or if a certain bill would be paid. Now I am blessed with not having to worry so much about those things. But I know I will be all right if I have to live that way again, because just as God was with us then, He is still with us today. He will see us through, be there for us, and catch us if He has to. He may even have to carry us as we walk along life's difficult path.

Yes, there may be days I will want to worry and fret, but on those days I will take heed and listen as God says, "Be still, and know that I am God. . . ." (Psalm 46:10). I will take my Bible out once more and read the forty-sixth chapter and then I will flip my Bible over to Matthew 6:25-27 and I will read:

"That is why I tell you not to worry about everyday life—whether you have enough food and drink, or enough clothes to wear. Isn't life more than food, and your body more than clothing? Look at the birds. They don't plant or harvest or store food in barns, for your heavenly Father feeds them. And aren't you far more valuable to Him than they are? Can all your worries add a single moment to your life?"

Then I can rest in the knowledge that God is my refuge and strength, and He will be ready to help me in my troubled times. I know where my help will come from, do you?

"For you are my hiding place; you protect me from trouble. You surround me with songs of victory."

Psalm 32:7

"The Lord is a shelter for the oppressed, a refuge in times of trouble."

Psalm 9:9

Prayer: Dear Lord, it is only human for me to fret and worry. I worry even in times of peace. I often wonder how long it will be before bad times hit again. In these days of rushing, it's hard to be still. In the arena of life, it is hard to hear your voice; I hear the distractions for my attention, but I can't hear you. Some have lost jobs, income, family, and friends. For some have lost all they owned. In these times of loss, worries, and stress, help me to hear your voice and be still. Open my heart to know you are God, and you can do all things if I just allow you to move in my life. Deliver me from worry and torment and replace those things with peace and assurance that you are in control of my life; for it is not in material things I find peace, but in you. Thank you for being the solid rock and being my hiding place in times of trouble. Amen.

Bear One Another's Burdens

Galatians 6:2, Romans 15:1

One of the many things I do every morning is ask God to use me. I pray also that I be filled with the Holy Spirit and be open to where He leads me. I pray that everything I say and do be pleasing unto Him. Now, having said that, I am not telling you this to make you think more highly of me; I am telling you this so you can see how God works. When we are open to God using us, when we are *willing* to be used by Him, we can help others along the way. Let me share.

One Monday morning, I was going to a shopping center to make a DVD of some pictures I wanted to share with others. When I arrived, I found two women working on the machines, so I had to wait my turn. After several minutes, I became impatient. I just had a five-minute job to do. These women were taking forever. One woman was a young lady in her early 20s or late teens. I could see over her shoulder that she was copying off pictures of a guy; probably a boyfriend. She was very slow and much focused. I just wanted her to finish, so I could get on with my day. Finally, after a few more minutes, she finished. Instead of leaving, she stood by the machine looking at each picture. I didn't step up, because I didn't want to seem rude or impatient (now isn't that a joke?). She turned and looked at me. I told her all I wanted to do was make a DVD. She suggested I go ahead. As I was beginning, she started to talk to me. I found out she was taking pictures off of her camera. The pictures she was getting were of a young man—her friend. This young friend of hers had just committed suicide on the Friday before. She was taking pictures of him off her camera to take to his mom. She would give them to her at the funeral later that day. I thought I hadn't heard right. She repeated herself. I stepped aside and told her to please finish her job as it was much more important than what I was doing. Instead of stepping away I felt like I needed to stay there with her. She continued talking and sharing with me. I told her I had a brother who had committed suicide, only by a different means. I told her I would be praying for her and his family. We spent the next few minutes sharing. God was among us, I am sure.

Afterward, I thought I should have gotten this girl's name and phone number. I should have done more. I should have stepped forward and paid for the pictures. I should have, I should have, but I know now I did what I was called to do. I prayed. I prayed for the next several days. I will continue to pray.

A few days later, a couple joined our church. The week before they joined, our minister had asked for prayer for this couple. They had just lost a grandson. I came to find out it was the same young man. I have not had the opportunity yet to share with them, but I do know in God's time it will happen.

The amazing thing was that, as I stepped up to the machine to make my DVD, it occurred to me that I wasn't thinking that morning. I could have made that DVD from my own computer at home. I believe God jumbled my thoughts, because He knew I would be needed. This young lady needed to share and I was open to her sharing with me. She would need prayer to help her through that afternoon, and I was a willing vessel able to pray for her and her family at the appointed time.

When we are open and willing to be used by God and for God, things happen. He will bring people and circumstances into our lives; people who need a touch, a shoulder to cry on or maybe we are just to listen as they grieve. It says in Galatians 6:2, "*Bear one another's burdens, and thereby fulfill the law of Christ"* (NASB). In Romans 15:1, it says, *"Now we who are strong ought to bear the weaknesses of those without strength and not just please ourselves"* (NASB).

I remember my brother's funeral. It was a difficult time. I am sure that young woman had a difficult afternoon. I knew I needed to ask God to give her and the family of the young man strength to get through these dark times. God had put me there for this reason: to pray. What struck me is anybody could have been there, but God put me there. By my going through my brother's suicide I could sympathize with her; I knew what she was feeling.

What I realize now is that I have to be open at all times if I am going to serve God. I have to be ready to share God's love, mercy, and grace with others. I have to be ready because just like this time, I may never know when I am needed. This may just be a once-in-a lifetime happening or God may once again put me in a situation with someone who needs His love.

The prayer I pray every morning has taken on new meaning. I am open to what God has planned for me and yes, I am willing to be used by God for God. How about you? Are you willing to be used? Are you ready to respond with God's love at a moment's notice? Be ready: You may not know the time, or the date or the circumstance; but if you are willing, God will use you just as He has me. May God bless you.

"Anyone who does the will of my Father in heaven is my brother and sister and mother!"

Matthew 12:50

"Don't forget to show hospitality to strangers, for some who have done this have entertained angels without realizing it!"

Hebrews 13:2

L.T. FROG

Prayer: Lord, you call me into service each day. Sometimes I respond and other times I am in too much of a hurry to hear your voice. You put others in my path who needs to know your love, mercy, and grace. Open my eyes to those around me who need to be touched by you. Help me to respond to those who are reaching out and teach me to be open to those who are hurting. May I always be willing to be used by you, for you, and through you. Amen.

References

Ortberg, John, *If You Want To Walk on Water, You've Got to Get Out Of the Boat*. Zondervan. Grand Rapids, Michigan.

Saint, Steve, *End of the Spear*. Tyndale House Publishers. Carol Stream, Illinois

CPSIA information can be obtained at www.ICGtesting.com
Printed in the USA
LVOW071449141212

311708LV00004B/112/P